ESTD 1982

HIGH QUALITY

WINE

TASTING JOURNAL

Pg.	🍷 NAME	🍾 WINERY	💵 PRICE	OVERALL RATING
01				☆☆☆☆☆
02				☆☆☆☆☆
03				☆☆☆☆☆
04				☆☆☆☆☆
05				☆☆☆☆☆
06				☆☆☆☆☆
07				☆☆☆☆☆
08				☆☆☆☆☆
09				☆☆☆☆☆
10				☆☆☆☆☆
11				☆☆☆☆☆
12				☆☆☆☆☆
13				☆☆☆☆☆
14				☆☆☆☆☆
15				☆☆☆☆☆
16				☆☆☆☆☆
17				☆☆☆☆☆
18				☆☆☆☆☆
19				☆☆☆☆☆
20				☆☆☆☆☆
21				☆☆☆☆☆
22				☆☆☆☆☆
23				☆☆☆☆☆
24				☆☆☆☆☆
25				☆☆☆☆☆
26				☆☆☆☆☆
27				☆☆☆☆☆

Pg.	🍷 NAME	🍾 WINERY	💵 PRICE	OVERALL RATING
28				☆☆☆☆☆
29				☆☆☆☆☆
30				☆☆☆☆☆
31				☆☆☆☆☆
32				☆☆☆☆☆
33				☆☆☆☆☆
34				☆☆☆☆☆
35				☆☆☆☆☆
36				☆☆☆☆☆
37				☆☆☆☆☆
38				☆☆☆☆☆
39				☆☆☆☆☆
40				☆☆☆☆☆
41				☆☆☆☆☆
42				☆☆☆☆☆
43				☆☆☆☆☆
44				☆☆☆☆☆
45				☆☆☆☆☆
46				☆☆☆☆☆
47				☆☆☆☆☆
48				☆☆☆☆☆
49				☆☆☆☆☆
50				☆☆☆☆☆
51				☆☆☆☆☆
52				☆☆☆☆☆
53				☆☆☆☆☆
54				☆☆☆☆☆

Pg.	NAME	WINERY	PRICE	OVERALL RATING
55				☆☆☆☆☆
56				☆☆☆☆☆
57				☆☆☆☆☆
58				☆☆☆☆☆
59				☆☆☆☆☆
60				☆☆☆☆☆
61				☆☆☆☆☆
62				☆☆☆☆☆
63				☆☆☆☆☆
64				☆☆☆☆☆
65				☆☆☆☆☆
66				☆☆☆☆☆
67				☆☆☆☆☆
68				☆☆☆☆☆
69				☆☆☆☆☆
70				☆☆☆☆☆
71				☆☆☆☆☆
72				☆☆☆☆☆
73				☆☆☆☆☆
74				☆☆☆☆☆
75				☆☆☆☆☆
76				☆☆☆☆☆
77				☆☆☆☆☆
78				☆☆☆☆☆
79				☆☆☆☆☆
80				☆☆☆☆☆
81				☆☆☆☆☆

Pg.	🍷 NAME	🍾 WINERY	💵 PRICE	OVERALL RATING
82				☆☆☆☆☆
83				☆☆☆☆☆
84				☆☆☆☆☆
85				☆☆☆☆☆
86				☆☆☆☆☆
87				☆☆☆☆☆
88				☆☆☆☆☆
89				☆☆☆☆☆
90				☆☆☆☆☆
91				☆☆☆☆☆
92				☆☆☆☆☆
93				☆☆☆☆☆
94				☆☆☆☆☆
95				☆☆☆☆☆
96				☆☆☆☆☆
97				☆☆☆☆☆
98				☆☆☆☆☆
99				☆☆☆☆☆
100				☆☆☆☆☆
101				☆☆☆☆☆
102				☆☆☆☆☆
103				☆☆☆☆☆
104				☆☆☆☆☆
105				☆☆☆☆☆
106				☆☆☆☆☆
107				☆☆☆☆☆
108				☆☆☆☆☆

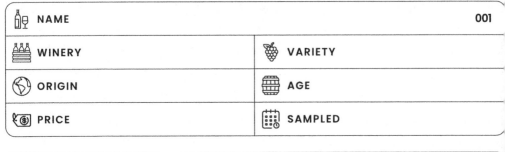

🍷 **NAME**		001
🍾 **WINERY**	🍇 **VARIETY**	
🌐 **ORIGIN**	🛢 **AGE**	
💵 **PRICE**	📅 **SAMPLED**	

COLOR METER

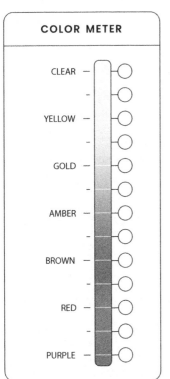

CLEAR —
-
YELLOW —
-
GOLD —
-
AMBER —
-
BROWN —
-
RED —
-
PURPLE —

AROMA AND FLAVOR WHEEL

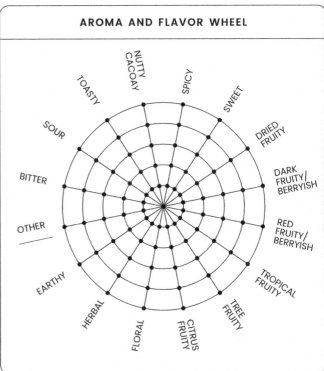

NUTTY CACOAY · SPICY · SWEET · DRIED FRUITY · DARK FRUITY/BERRYISH · RED FRUITY/BERRYISH · TROPICAL FRUITY · TREE FRUITY · CITRUS FRUITY · FLORAL · HERBAL · EARTHY · OTHER · BITTER · SOUR · TOASTY

NOTES AND RATING

🔍 APPEARANCE	☆☆☆☆☆
👃 AROMA	☆☆☆☆☆
🍷 FLAVOR	☆☆☆☆☆
✍ OVERALL RATING	☆☆☆☆☆

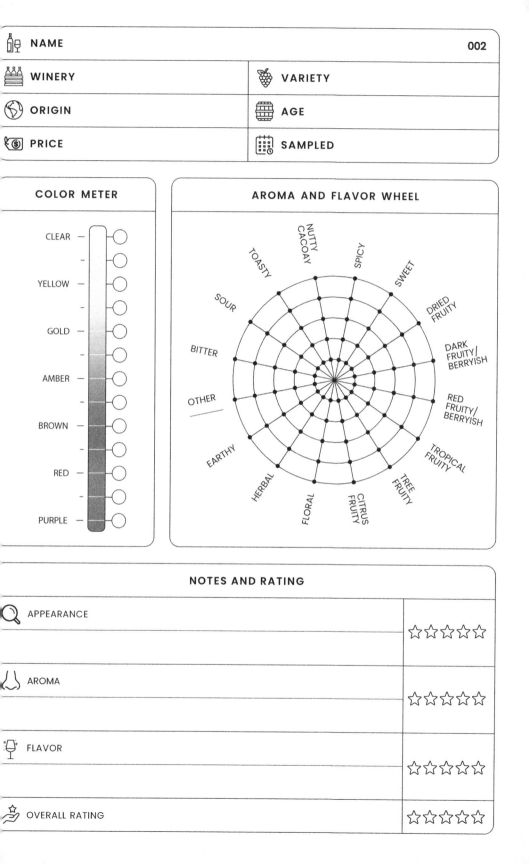 NAME		002
WINERY	VARIETY	
ORIGIN	AGE	
PRICE	SAMPLED	

COLOR METER

- CLEAR
- —
- YELLOW
- —
- GOLD
- —
- AMBER
- —
- BROWN
- —
- RED
- —
- PURPLE

AROMA AND FLAVOR WHEEL

NUTTY CACOAY
TOASTY
SPICY
SOUR
SWEET
BITTER
DRIED FRUITY
OTHER
DARK FRUITY/ BERRYISH
EARTHY
RED FRUITY/ BERRYISH
HERBAL
TROPICAL FRUITY
FLORAL
TREE FRUITY
CITRUS FRUITY

NOTES AND RATING

APPEARANCE	☆☆☆☆☆
AROMA	☆☆☆☆☆
FLAVOR	☆☆☆☆☆
OVERALL RATING	☆☆☆☆☆

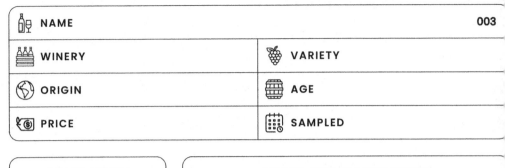

🍷 NAME	003

🍾 WINERY	🍇 VARIETY
🌍 ORIGIN	🛢️ AGE
💵 PRICE	📅 SAMPLED

COLOR METER

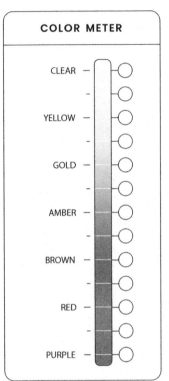

CLEAR —
—
YELLOW —
—
GOLD —
—
AMBER —
—
BROWN —
—
RED —
—
PURPLE —

AROMA AND FLAVOR WHEEL

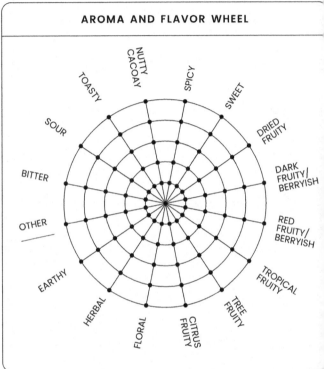

NUTTY CACOAY
SPICY
TOASTY
SWEET
SOUR
DRIED FRUITY
BITTER
DARK FRUITY/ BERRYISH
OTHER
RED FRUITY/ BERRYISH
EARTHY
TROPICAL FRUITY
HERBAL
TREE FRUITY
FLORAL
CITRUS FRUITY

NOTES AND RATING

🔍 APPEARANCE	☆☆☆☆☆
👃 AROMA	☆☆☆☆☆
🍷 FLAVOR	☆☆☆☆☆
🤲 OVERALL RATING	☆☆☆☆☆

🍾 **NAME**		004

🍷 **WINERY**	🍇 **VARIETY**
🌍 **ORIGIN**	🛢 **AGE**
💰 **PRICE**	📅 **SAMPLED**

COLOR METER

- CLEAR —
- —
- YELLOW —
- —
- GOLD —
- —
- AMBER —
- —
- BROWN —
- —
- RED —
- —
- PURPLE —

AROMA AND FLAVOR WHEEL

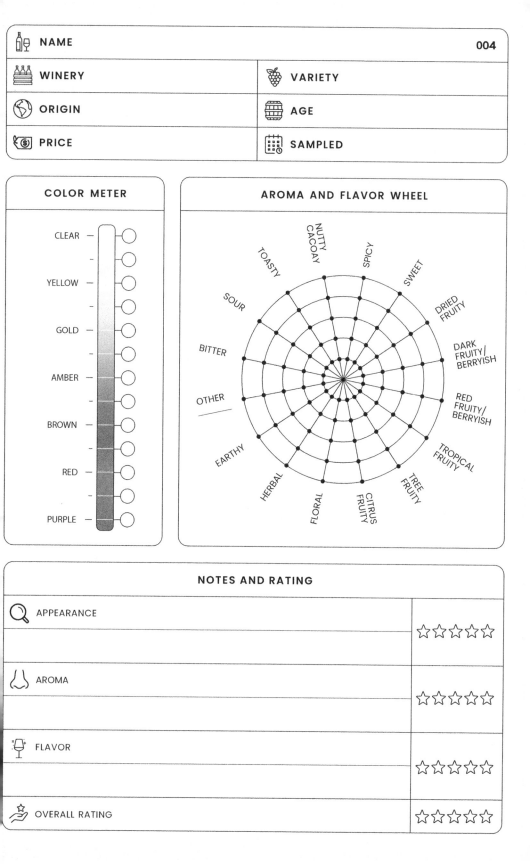

NUTTY CACOAY · SPICY · SWEET · DRIED FRUITY · DARK FRUITY/BERRYISH · RED FRUITY/BERRYISH · TROPICAL FRUITY · TREE FRUITY · CITRUS FRUITY · FLORAL · HERBAL · EARTHY · OTHER · BITTER · SOUR · TOASTY

NOTES AND RATING

🔍 **APPEARANCE**	☆☆☆☆☆
👃 **AROMA**	☆☆☆☆☆
🍷 **FLAVOR**	☆☆☆☆☆
🏆 **OVERALL RATING**	☆☆☆☆☆

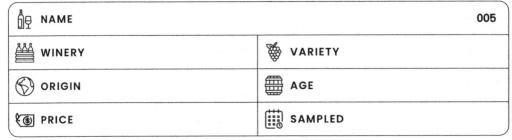

🍾 NAME	005
🍾 WINERY	🍇 VARIETY
🌍 ORIGIN	🛢 AGE
💲 PRICE	📅 SAMPLED

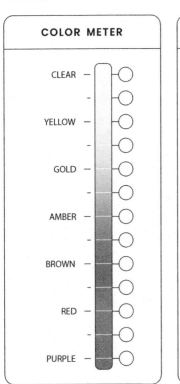

COLOR METER

CLEAR —
-
YELLOW —
-
GOLD —
-
AMBER —
-
BROWN —
-
RED —
-
PURPLE —

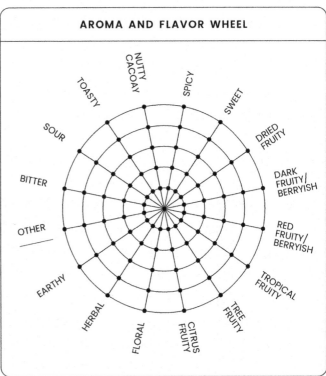

AROMA AND FLAVOR WHEEL

NUTTY CACOAY
TOASTY
SPICY
SOUR
SWEET
BITTER
DRIED FRUITY
OTHER
DARK FRUITY/ BERRYISH
RED FRUITY/ BERRYISH
EARTHY
TROPICAL FRUITY
HERBAL
TREE FRUITY
FLORAL
CITRUS FRUITY

NOTES AND RATING

🔍 APPEARANCE	☆☆☆☆☆
👃 AROMA	☆☆☆☆☆
🍷 FLAVOR	☆☆☆☆☆
🤲 OVERALL RATING	☆☆☆☆☆

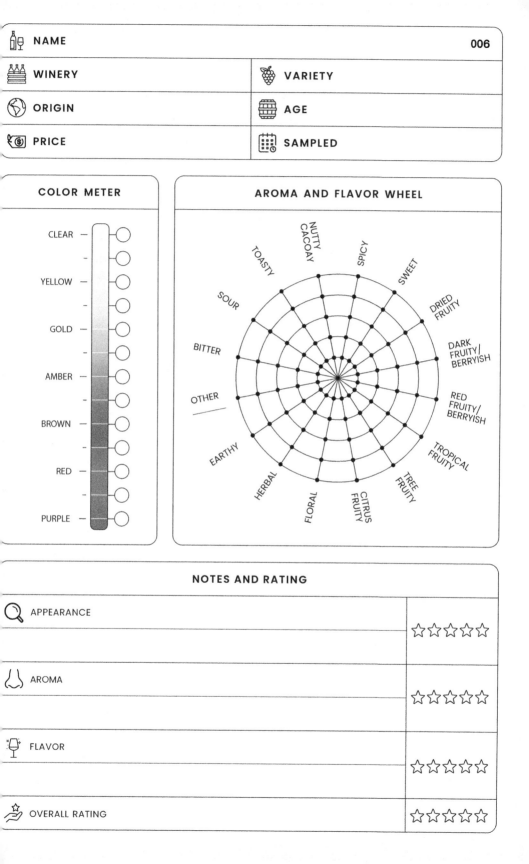

NAME

WINERY

VARIETY

ORIGIN

AGE

PRICE

SAMPLED

COLOR METER

CLEAR

—

YELLOW

—

GOLD

—

AMBER

—

BROWN

—

RED

—

PURPLE

AROMA AND FLAVOR WHEEL

NUTTY CACOAY
TOASTY
SPICY
SOUR
SWEET
BITTER
DRIED FRUITY
OTHER
DARK FRUITY/ BERRYISH
RED FRUITY/ BERRYISH
EARTHY
TROPICAL FRUITY
HERBAL
TREE FRUITY
FLORAL
CITRUS FRUITY

NOTES AND RATING

APPEARANCE

☆☆☆☆☆

AROMA

☆☆☆☆☆

FLAVOR

☆☆☆☆☆

OVERALL RATING

☆☆☆☆☆

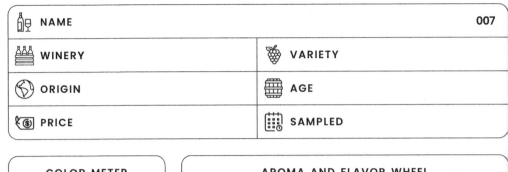

🍷 NAME	007
🍾 WINERY	🍇 VARIETY
🌐 ORIGIN	🛢 AGE
💵 PRICE	📅 SAMPLED

COLOR METER

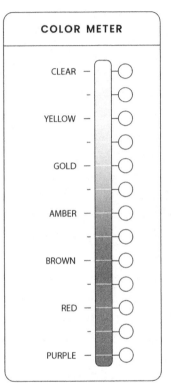

CLEAR —
—
YELLOW —
—
GOLD —
—
AMBER —
—
BROWN —
—
RED —
—
PURPLE —

AROMA AND FLAVOR WHEEL

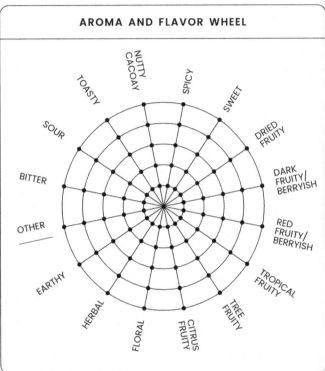

NUTTY CACOAY
TOASTY
SPICY
SWEET
SOUR
DRIED FRUITY
BITTER
DARK FRUITY/ BERRYISH
OTHER
RED FRUITY/ BERRYISH
EARTHY
TROPICAL FRUITY
HERBAL
TREE FRUITY
FLORAL
CITRUS FRUITY

NOTES AND RATING

🔍 APPEARANCE	☆☆☆☆☆
👃 AROMA	☆☆☆☆☆
🍷 FLAVOR	☆☆☆☆☆
🖐 OVERALL RATING	☆☆☆☆☆

NAME

WINERY		VARIETY	
ORIGIN		AGE	
PRICE		SAMPLED	

COLOR METER

CLEAR —
–
YELLOW —
–
GOLD —
–
AMBER —
–
BROWN —
–
RED —
–
PURPLE —

AROMA AND FLAVOR WHEEL

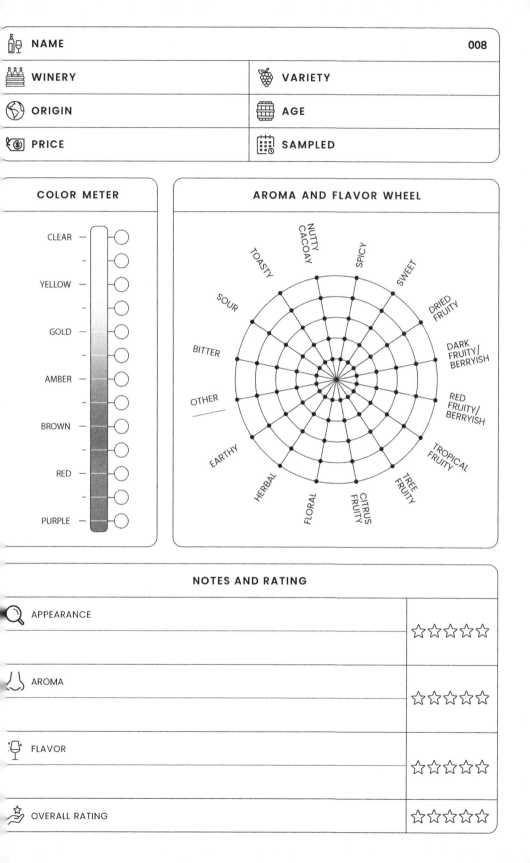

NUTTY CACOAY
TOASTY
SPICY
SOUR
SWEET
DRIED FRUITY
BITTER
DARK FRUITY/BERRYISH
OTHER
RED FRUITY/BERRYISH
EARTHY
TROPICAL FRUITY
HERBAL
TREE FRUITY
FLORAL
CITRUS FRUITY

NOTES AND RATING

APPEARANCE ☆☆☆☆☆

AROMA ☆☆☆☆☆

FLAVOR ☆☆☆☆☆

OVERALL RATING ☆☆☆☆☆

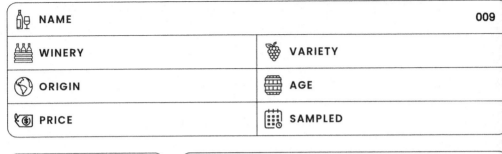

NAME	
WINERY	VARIETY
ORIGIN	AGE
PRICE	SAMPLED

COLOR METER

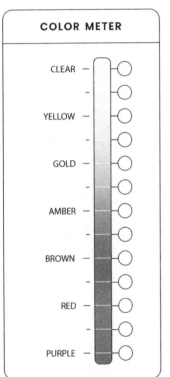

- CLEAR
- –
- YELLOW
- –
- GOLD
- –
- AMBER
- –
- BROWN
- –
- RED
- –
- PURPLE

AROMA AND FLAVOR WHEEL

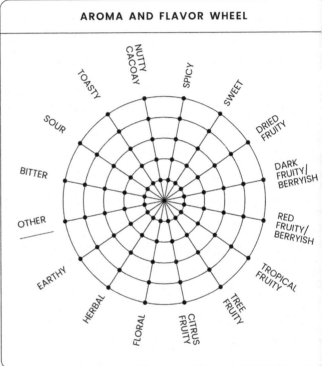

NUTTY CACOAY · SPICY · SWEET · DRIED FRUITY · DARK FRUITY/BERRYISH · RED FRUITY/BERRYISH · TROPICAL FRUITY · TREE FRUITY · CITRUS FRUITY · FLORAL · HERBAL · EARTHY · OTHER · BITTER · SOUR · TOASTY

NOTES AND RATING

APPEARANCE	☆☆☆☆☆
AROMA	☆☆☆☆☆
FLAVOR	☆☆☆☆☆
OVERALL RATING	☆☆☆☆☆

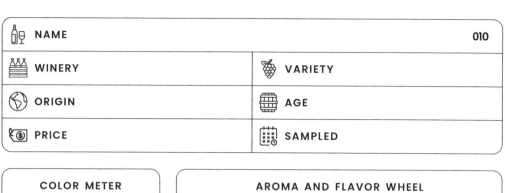

🍷 NAME	010
🍾 WINERY	🍇 VARIETY
🌍 ORIGIN	🛢 AGE
💲 PRICE	📅 SAMPLED

COLOR METER

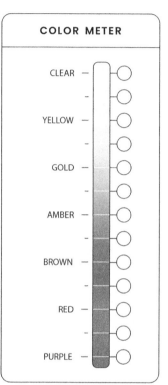

CLEAR —

—

YELLOW —

—

GOLD —

—

AMBER —

—

BROWN —

—

RED —

—

PURPLE —

AROMA AND FLAVOR WHEEL

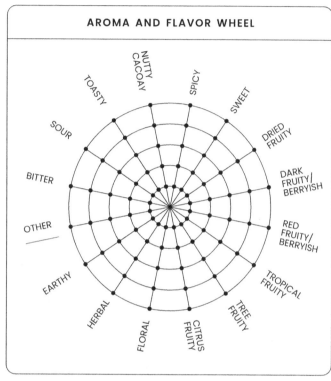

NUTTY CACOAY · SPICY · SWEET · DRIED FRUITY · DARK FRUITY/BERRYISH · RED FRUITY/BERRYISH · TROPICAL FRUITY · TREE FRUITY · CITRUS FRUITY · FLORAL · HERBAL · EARTHY · OTHER · BITTER · SOUR · TOASTY

NOTES AND RATING

🔍 APPEARANCE

☆☆☆☆☆

👃 AROMA

☆☆☆☆☆

🍷 FLAVOR

☆☆☆☆☆

🤲 OVERALL RATING

☆☆☆☆☆

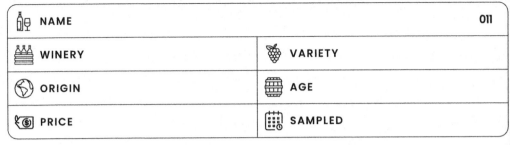

🍾 **NAME**		011
🍷 **WINERY**	🍇 **VARIETY**	
🌍 **ORIGIN**	🛢 **AGE**	
💵 **PRICE**	📅 **SAMPLED**	

COLOR METER

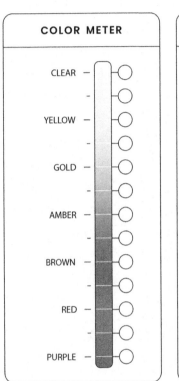

CLEAR
–
YELLOW
–
GOLD
–
AMBER
–
BROWN
–
RED
–
PURPLE

AROMA AND FLAVOR WHEEL

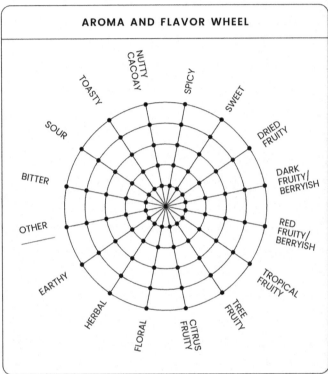

NUTTY CACOAY · SPICY · SWEET · DRIED FRUITY · DARK FRUITY/BERRYISH · RED FRUITY/BERRYISH · TROPICAL FRUITY · TREE FRUITY · CITRUS FRUITY · FLORAL · HERBAL · EARTHY · OTHER · BITTER · SOUR · TOASTY

NOTES AND RATING

🔍 APPEARANCE	☆☆☆☆☆
👃 AROMA	☆☆☆☆☆
🍷 FLAVOR	☆☆☆☆☆
🤲 OVERALL RATING	☆☆☆☆☆

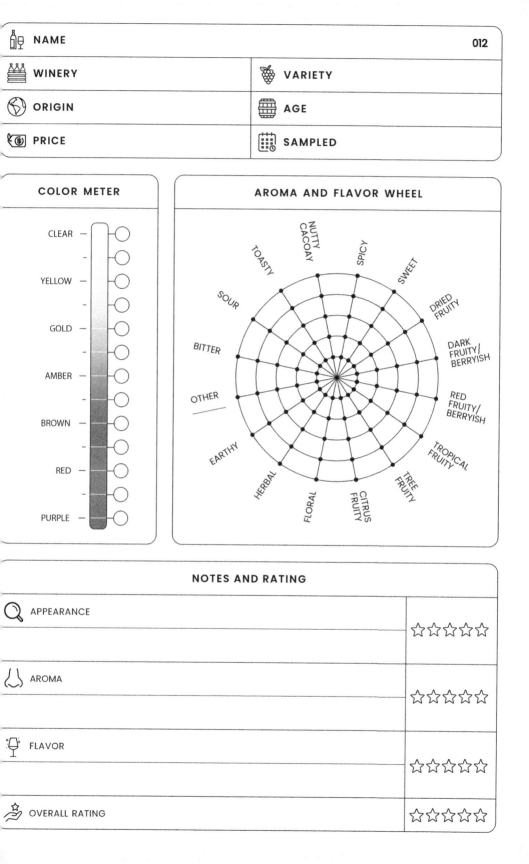 NAME	
WINERY	VARIETY
ORIGIN	AGE
PRICE	SAMPLED

COLOR METER

- CLEAR
- YELLOW
- GOLD
- AMBER
- BROWN
- RED
- PURPLE

AROMA AND FLAVOR WHEEL

NUTTY CACOAY · SPICY · SWEET · DRIED FRUITY · DARK FRUITY / BERRYISH · RED FRUITY / BERRYISH · TROPICAL FRUITY · TREE FRUITY · CITRUS FRUITY · FLORAL · HERBAL · EARTHY · OTHER · BITTER · SOUR · TOASTY

NOTES AND RATING

APPEARANCE	☆☆☆☆☆
AROMA	☆☆☆☆☆
FLAVOR	☆☆☆☆☆
OVERALL RATING	☆☆☆☆☆

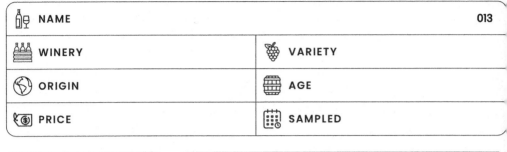

🍾 NAME	013
🍾 WINERY	🍇 VARIETY
🌍 ORIGIN	🛢 AGE
💵 PRICE	📅 SAMPLED

COLOR METER

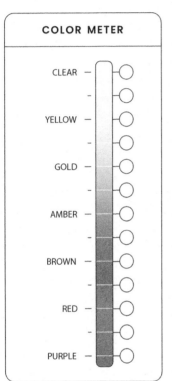

CLEAR

YELLOW

GOLD

AMBER

BROWN

RED

PURPLE

AROMA AND FLAVOR WHEEL

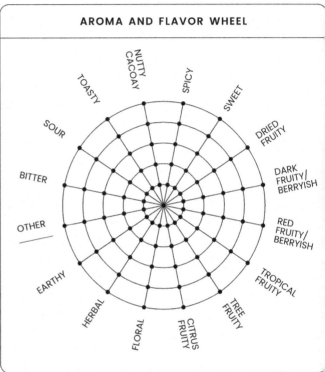

NUTTY CACOAY — SPICY — SWEET — TOASTY — SOUR — DRIED FRUITY — BITTER — DARK FRUITY/BERRYISH — OTHER — RED FRUITY/BERRYISH — EARTHY — TROPICAL FRUITY — HERBAL — FLORAL — CITRUS FRUITY — TREE FRUITY

NOTES AND RATING

🔍 APPEARANCE	☆☆☆☆☆
👃 AROMA	☆☆☆☆☆
🍷 FLAVOR	☆☆☆☆☆
🖐 OVERALL RATING	☆☆☆☆☆

NAME

WINERY	VARIETY
ORIGIN	AGE
PRICE	SAMPLED

COLOR METER

CLEAR —

—

YELLOW —

—

GOLD —

—

AMBER —

—

BROWN —

—

RED —

—

PURPLE —

AROMA AND FLAVOR WHEEL

NUTTY CACOAY
TOASTY
SPICY
SOUR
SWEET
BITTER
DRIED FRUITY
OTHER
DARK FRUITY/ BERRYISH
EARTHY
RED FRUITY/ BERRYISH
HERBAL
TROPICAL FRUITY
FLORAL
TREE FRUITY
CITRUS FRUITY

NOTES AND RATING

APPEARANCE

☆☆☆☆☆

AROMA

☆☆☆☆☆

FLAVOR

☆☆☆☆☆

OVERALL RATING

☆☆☆☆☆

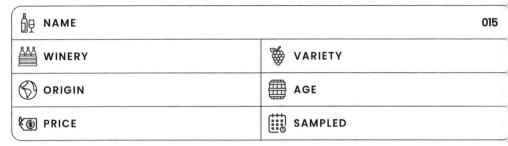

 🍾 NAME	015
🍾 WINERY	🍇 VARIETY
🌍 ORIGIN	🛢 AGE
💵 PRICE	📅 SAMPLED

COLOR METER

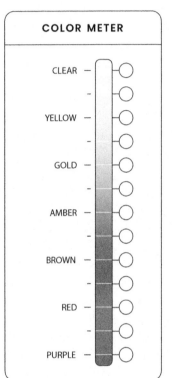

CLEAR —

YELLOW —

GOLD —

AMBER —

BROWN —

RED —

PURPLE —

AROMA AND FLAVOR WHEEL

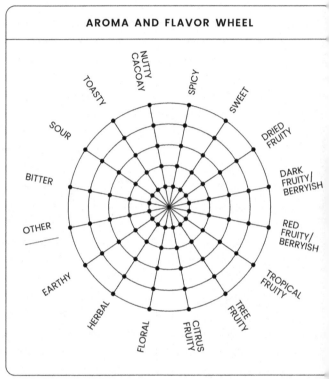

NUTTY CACOAY · SPICY · SWEET · DRIED FRUITY · DARK FRUITY/BERRYISH · RED FRUITY/BERRYISH · TROPICAL FRUITY · TREE FRUITY · CITRUS FRUITY · FLORAL · HERBAL · EARTHY · OTHER · BITTER · SOUR · TOASTY

NOTES AND RATING

🔍 APPEARANCE

☆☆☆☆☆

👃 AROMA

☆☆☆☆☆

🍷 FLAVOR

☆☆☆☆☆

🤲 OVERALL RATING

☆☆☆☆☆

🍾 **NAME**		016
🍷 **WINERY**	🍇 **VARIETY**	
🌏 **ORIGIN**	🛢 **AGE**	
💲 **PRICE**	📅 **SAMPLED**	

COLOR METER

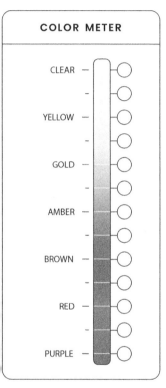

CLEAR
–
YELLOW
–
GOLD
–
AMBER
–
BROWN
–
RED
–
PURPLE

AROMA AND FLAVOR WHEEL

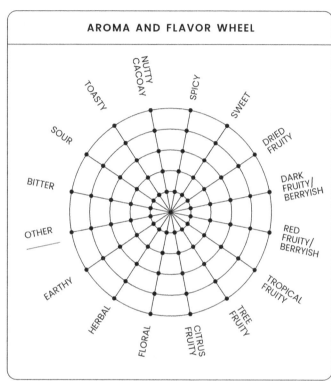

NUTTY CACOAY · SPICY · SWEET · DRIED FRUITY · DARK FRUITY/BERRYISH · RED FRUITY/BERRYISH · TROPICAL FRUITY · TREE FRUITY · CITRUS FRUITY · FLORAL · HERBAL · EARTHY · OTHER · BITTER · SOUR · TOASTY

NOTES AND RATING

🔍 APPEARANCE	☆☆☆☆☆
👃 AROMA	☆☆☆☆☆
🍷 FLAVOR	☆☆☆☆☆
🤲 OVERALL RATING	☆☆☆☆☆

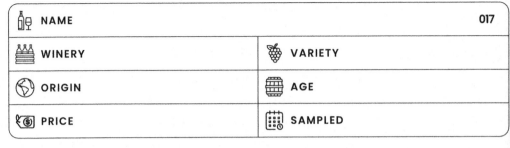

NAME	017

WINERY	VARIETY
ORIGIN	AGE
PRICE	SAMPLED

COLOR METER

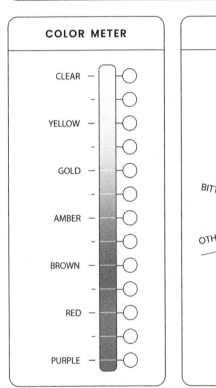

CLEAR

YELLOW

GOLD

AMBER

BROWN

RED

PURPLE

AROMA AND FLAVOR WHEEL

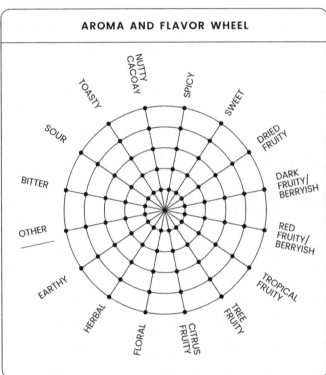

NUTTY CACOAY
SPICY
TOASTY
SWEET
SOUR
DRIED FRUITY
BITTER
DARK FRUITY/ BERRYISH
OTHER
RED FRUITY/ BERRYISH
EARTHY
TROPICAL FRUITY
HERBAL
TREE FRUITY
FLORAL
CITRUS FRUITY

NOTES AND RATING

APPEARANCE	☆☆☆☆☆
AROMA	☆☆☆☆☆
FLAVOR	☆☆☆☆☆
OVERALL RATING	☆☆☆☆☆

🍾 **NAME**		018

🍷 **WINERY**	🍇 **VARIETY**
🌍 **ORIGIN**	🛢 **AGE**
💰 **PRICE**	📅 **SAMPLED**

COLOR METER

- CLEAR —
- –
- YELLOW —
- –
- GOLD —
- –
- AMBER —
- –
- BROWN —
- –
- RED —
- –
- PURPLE —

AROMA AND FLAVOR WHEEL

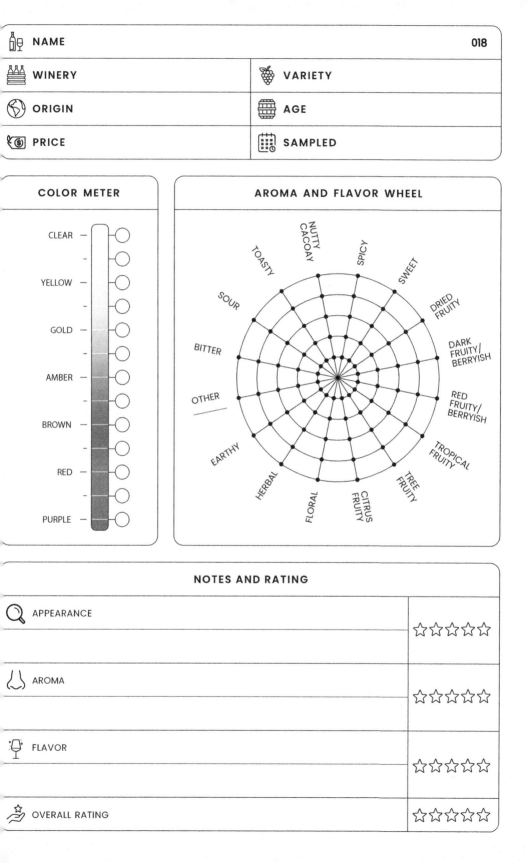

NUTTY CACOAY · TOASTY · SPICY · SOUR · SWEET · BITTER · DRIED FRUITY · DARK FRUITY/BERRYISH · OTHER · RED FRUITY/BERRYISH · EARTHY · TROPICAL FRUITY · HERBAL · FLORAL · CITRUS FRUITY · TREE FRUITY

NOTES AND RATING

🔍 **APPEARANCE**	☆☆☆☆☆
👃 **AROMA**	☆☆☆☆☆
🍷 **FLAVOR**	☆☆☆☆☆
🌟 **OVERALL RATING**	☆☆☆☆☆

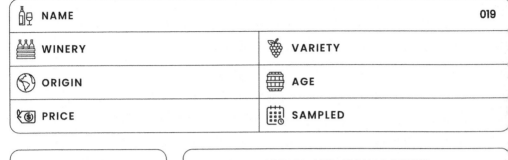

🍾 **NAME**		019
🍾 **WINERY**	🍇 **VARIETY**	
🌍 **ORIGIN**	🛢 **AGE**	
💵 **PRICE**	📅 **SAMPLED**	

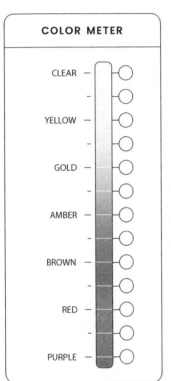

COLOR METER

- CLEAR
- –
- YELLOW
- –
- GOLD
- –
- AMBER
- –
- BROWN
- –
- RED
- –
- PURPLE

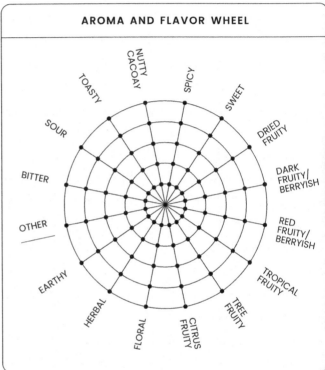

AROMA AND FLAVOR WHEEL

NUTTY CACOAY · SPICY · SWEET · DRIED FRUITY · DARK FRUITY/ BERRYISH · RED FRUITY/ BERRYISH · TROPICAL FRUITY · TREE FRUITY · CITRUS FRUITY · FLORAL · HERBAL · EARTHY · OTHER · BITTER · SOUR · TOASTY

NOTES AND RATING

🔍 APPEARANCE	☆☆☆☆☆
👃 AROMA	☆☆☆☆☆
🍷 FLAVOR	☆☆☆☆☆
🖐 OVERALL RATING	☆☆☆☆☆

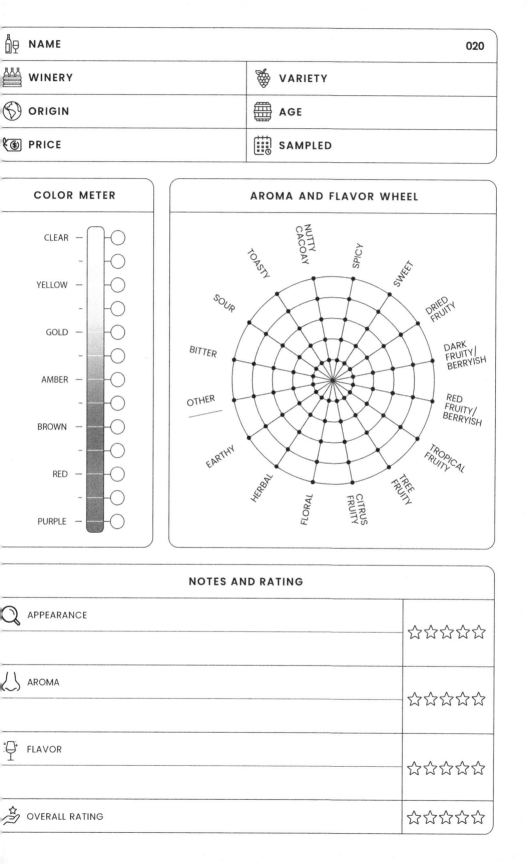

NAME

020

WINERY

VARIETY

ORIGIN

AGE

PRICE

SAMPLED

COLOR METER

CLEAR

YELLOW

GOLD

AMBER

BROWN

RED

PURPLE

AROMA AND FLAVOR WHEEL

NUTTY CACOAY

TOASTY

SPICY

SOUR

SWEET

BITTER

DRIED FRUITY

OTHER

DARK FRUITY/ BERRYISH

EARTHY

RED FRUITY/ BERRYISH

HERBAL

TROPICAL FRUITY

FLORAL

CITRUS FRUITY

TREE FRUITY

NOTES AND RATING

APPEARANCE

☆☆☆☆☆

AROMA

☆☆☆☆☆

FLAVOR

☆☆☆☆☆

OVERALL RATING

☆☆☆☆☆

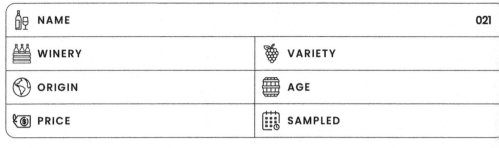

NAME

WINERY

VARIETY

ORIGIN

AGE

PRICE

SAMPLED

COLOR METER

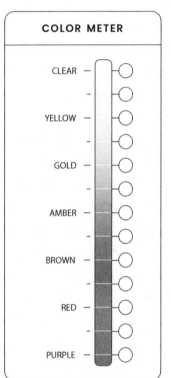

CLEAR

YELLOW

GOLD

AMBER

BROWN

RED

PURPLE

AROMA AND FLAVOR WHEEL

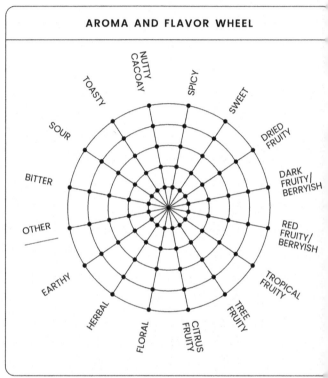

NUTTY CACOAY
TOASTY
SPICY
SWEET
SOUR
DRIED FRUITY
BITTER
DARK FRUITY/ BERRYISH
OTHER
RED FRUITY/ BERRYISH
EARTHY
TROPICAL FRUITY
HERBAL
TREE FRUITY
FLORAL
CITRUS FRUITY

NOTES AND RATING

APPEARANCE
☆☆☆☆☆

AROMA
☆☆☆☆☆

FLAVOR
☆☆☆☆☆

OVERALL RATING
☆☆☆☆☆

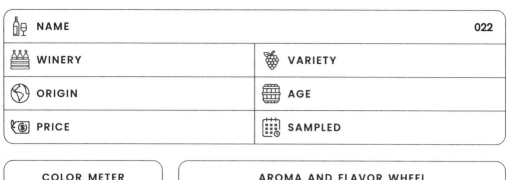

🍷 NAME	022
🍾 WINERY	🍇 VARIETY
🌍 ORIGIN	🛢 AGE
💲 PRICE	📅 SAMPLED

COLOR METER

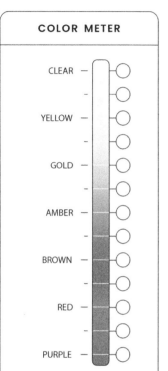

CLEAR —
—
YELLOW —
—
GOLD —
—
AMBER —
—
BROWN —
—
RED —
—
PURPLE —

AROMA AND FLAVOR WHEEL

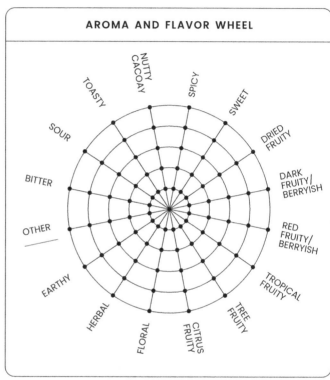

NUTTY CACOAY · SPICY · SWEET · DRIED FRUITY · DARK FRUITY/BERRYISH · RED FRUITY/BERRYISH · TROPICAL FRUITY · TREE FRUITY · CITRUS FRUITY · FLORAL · HERBAL · EARTHY · OTHER · BITTER · SOUR · TOASTY

NOTES AND RATING

🔍 APPEARANCE	☆☆☆☆☆
👃 AROMA	☆☆☆☆☆
🍷 FLAVOR	☆☆☆☆☆
🤲 OVERALL RATING	☆☆☆☆☆

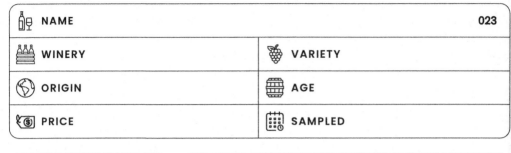

🍾 NAME	023
🍾 WINERY	🍇 VARIETY
🌍 ORIGIN	🛢 AGE
💵 PRICE	📅 SAMPLED

COLOR METER

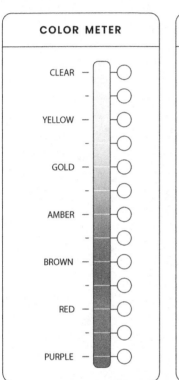

CLEAR —
—
YELLOW —
—
GOLD —
—
AMBER —
—
BROWN —
—
RED —
—
PURPLE —

AROMA AND FLAVOR WHEEL

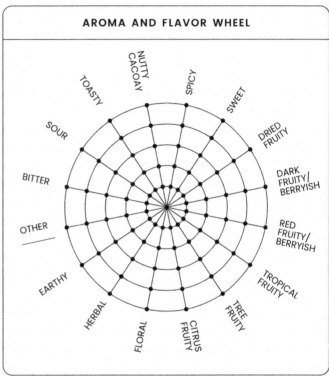

NUTTY CACOAY
SPICY
SWEET
DRIED FRUITY
DARK FRUITY/BERRYISH
RED FRUITY/BERRYISH
TROPICAL FRUITY
TREE FRUITY
CITRUS FRUITY
FLORAL
HERBAL
EARTHY
OTHER
BITTER
SOUR
TOASTY

NOTES AND RATING

🔍 APPEARANCE	☆☆☆☆☆
👃 AROMA	☆☆☆☆☆
🍷 FLAVOR	☆☆☆☆☆
🙌 OVERALL RATING	☆☆☆☆☆

NAME

WINERY

VARIETY

ORIGIN

AGE

PRICE

SAMPLED

COLOR METER

- CLEAR
- YELLOW
- GOLD
- AMBER
- BROWN
- RED
- PURPLE

AROMA AND FLAVOR WHEEL

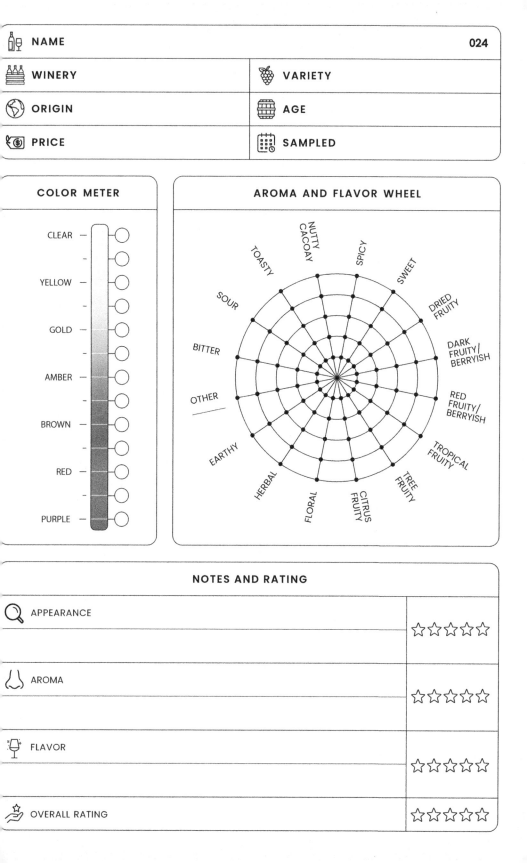

NUTTY CACOAY · SPICY · TOASTY · SWEET · SOUR · DRIED FRUITY · BITTER · DARK FRUITY / BERRYISH · OTHER · RED FRUITY / BERRYISH · EARTHY · TROPICAL FRUITY · HERBAL · TREE FRUITY · FLORAL · CITRUS FRUITY

NOTES AND RATING

APPEARANCE
☆☆☆☆☆

AROMA
☆☆☆☆☆

FLAVOR
☆☆☆☆☆

OVERALL RATING
☆☆☆☆☆

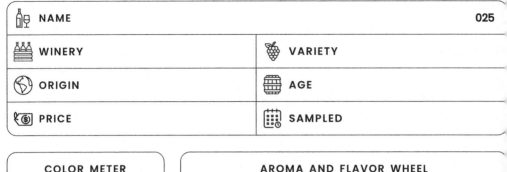 NAME		025
WINERY	VARIETY	
ORIGIN	AGE	
PRICE	SAMPLED	

COLOR METER

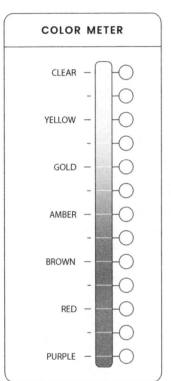

CLEAR
–
YELLOW
–
GOLD
–
AMBER
–
BROWN
–
RED
–
PURPLE

AROMA AND FLAVOR WHEEL

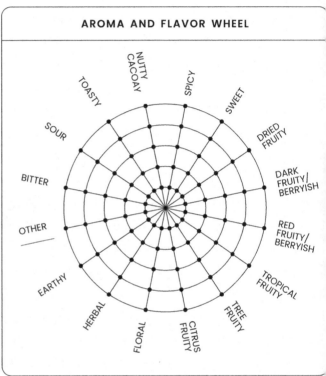

NUTTY CACOAY · SPICY · SWEET · DRIED FRUITY · DARK FRUITY/BERRYISH · RED FRUITY/BERRYISH · TROPICAL FRUITY · TREE FRUITY · CITRUS FRUITY · FLORAL · HERBAL · EARTHY · OTHER · BITTER · SOUR · TOASTY

NOTES AND RATING

APPEARANCE	☆☆☆☆☆
AROMA	☆☆☆☆☆
FLAVOR	☆☆☆☆☆
OVERALL RATING	☆☆☆☆☆

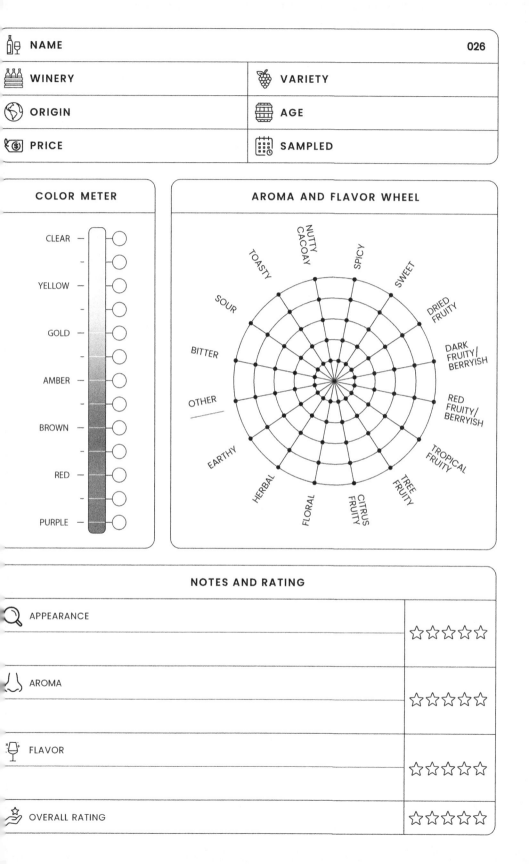

NAME

026

WINERY	VARIETY
ORIGIN	AGE
PRICE	SAMPLED

COLOR METER

- CLEAR
- YELLOW
- GOLD
- AMBER
- BROWN
- RED
- PURPLE

AROMA AND FLAVOR WHEEL

- NUTTY CACOAY
- SPICY
- TOASTY
- SWEET
- SOUR
- DRIED FRUITY
- BITTER
- DARK FRUITY/ BERRYISH
- OTHER
- RED FRUITY/ BERRYISH
- EARTHY
- TROPICAL FRUITY
- HERBAL
- TREE FRUITY
- FLORAL
- CITRUS FRUITY

NOTES AND RATING

APPEARANCE
☆☆☆☆☆

AROMA
☆☆☆☆☆

FLAVOR
☆☆☆☆☆

OVERALL RATING
☆☆☆☆☆

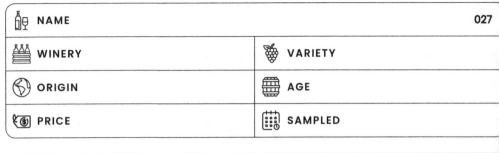

NAME 027

WINERY | **VARIETY**

ORIGIN | **AGE**

PRICE | **SAMPLED**

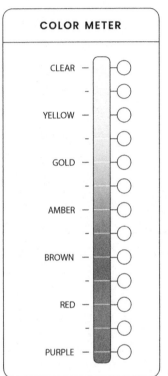

COLOR METER

CLEAR —
—
YELLOW —
—
GOLD —
—
AMBER —
—
BROWN —
—
RED —
—
PURPLE —

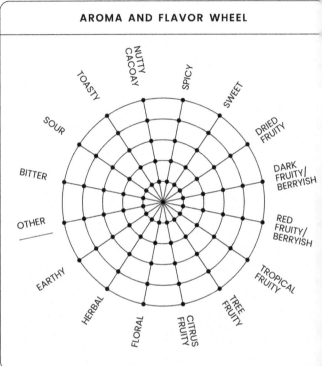

AROMA AND FLAVOR WHEEL

NUTTY CACOAY
SPICY
TOASTY
SWEET
SOUR
DRIED FRUITY
BITTER
DARK FRUITY/ BERRYISH
OTHER
RED FRUITY/ BERRYISH
EARTHY
TROPICAL FRUITY
HERBAL
TREE FRUITY
FLORAL
CITRUS FRUITY

NOTES AND RATING

APPEARANCE
☆☆☆☆☆

AROMA
☆☆☆☆☆

FLAVOR
☆☆☆☆☆

OVERALL RATING
☆☆☆☆☆

🍷 NAME	028

🍾 WINERY	🍇 VARIETY
🌍 ORIGIN	🛢 AGE
💲 PRICE	📅 SAMPLED

COLOR METER

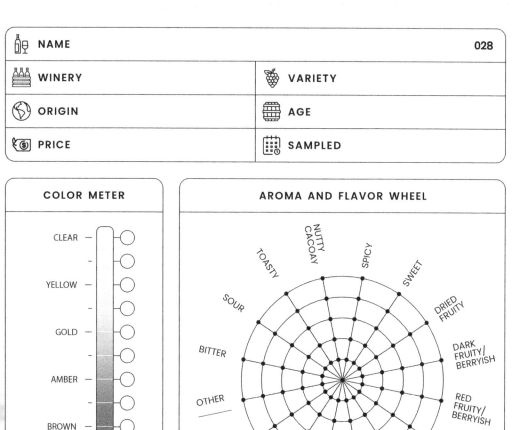

- CLEAR —
- —
- YELLOW —
- —
- GOLD —
- —
- AMBER —
- —
- BROWN —
- —
- RED —
- —
- PURPLE —

AROMA AND FLAVOR WHEEL

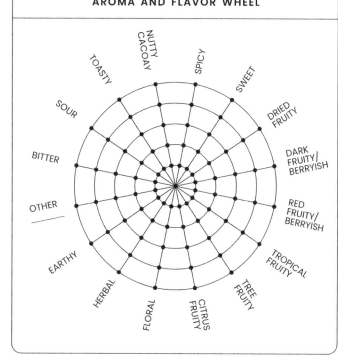

NUTTY CACOAY · SPICY · TOASTY · SWEET · SOUR · DRIED FRUITY · BITTER · DARK FRUITY/BERRYISH · OTHER · RED FRUITY/BERRYISH · EARTHY · TROPICAL FRUITY · HERBAL · TREE FRUITY · FLORAL · CITRUS FRUITY

NOTES AND RATING

🔍 APPEARANCE	☆☆☆☆☆
👃 AROMA	☆☆☆☆☆
🍷 FLAVOR	☆☆☆☆☆
🤲 OVERALL RATING	☆☆☆☆☆

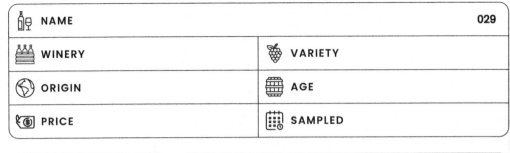

🍾 **NAME**	**029**
🍷 **WINERY**	🍇 **VARIETY**
🌐 **ORIGIN**	🛢 **AGE**
💵 **PRICE**	📅 **SAMPLED**

COLOR METER

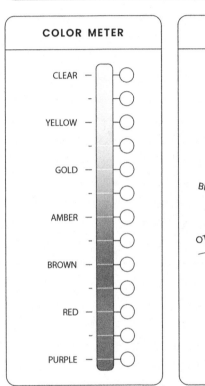

CLEAR —
-
YELLOW —
-
GOLD —
-
AMBER —
-
BROWN —
-
RED —
-
PURPLE —

AROMA AND FLAVOR WHEEL

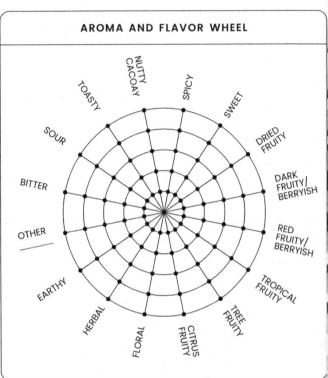

NUTTY CACOAY · SPICY · SWEET · DRIED FRUITY · DARK FRUITY/BERRYISH · RED FRUITY/BERRYISH · TROPICAL FRUITY · TREE FRUITY · CITRUS FRUITY · FLORAL · HERBAL · EARTHY · OTHER · BITTER · SOUR · TOASTY

NOTES AND RATING

🔍 APPEARANCE	☆☆☆☆☆
👃 AROMA	☆☆☆☆☆
🍷 FLAVOR	☆☆☆☆☆
🖐 OVERALL RATING	☆☆☆☆☆

NAME

WINERY	**VARIETY**
ORIGIN	**AGE**
PRICE	**SAMPLED**

COLOR METER

- CLEAR
- —
- YELLOW
- —
- GOLD
- —
- AMBER
- —
- BROWN
- —
- RED
- —
- PURPLE

AROMA AND FLAVOR WHEEL

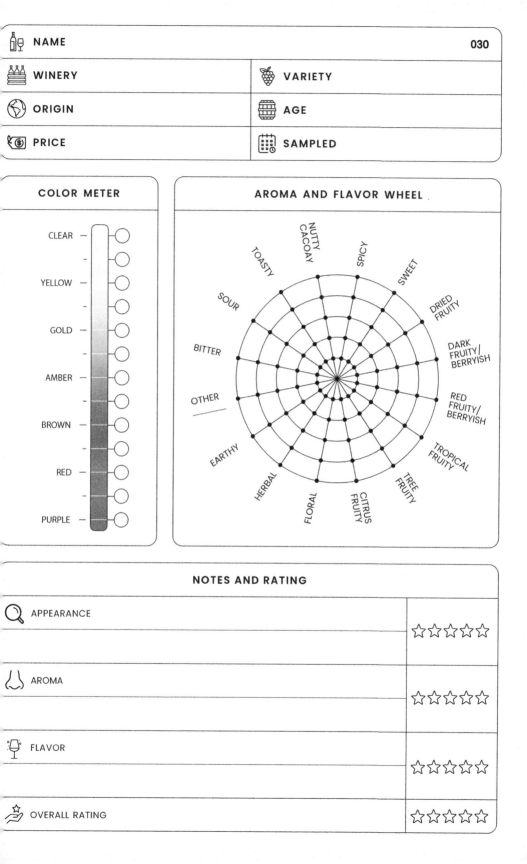

NUTTY CACOAY · SPICY · SWEET · DRIED FRUITY · DARK FRUITY / BERRYISH · RED FRUITY / BERRYISH · TROPICAL FRUITY · TREE FRUITY · CITRUS FRUITY · FLORAL · HERBAL · EARTHY · OTHER · BITTER · SOUR · TOASTY

NOTES AND RATING

APPEARANCE

☆☆☆☆☆

AROMA

☆☆☆☆☆

FLAVOR

☆☆☆☆☆

OVERALL RATING

☆☆☆☆☆

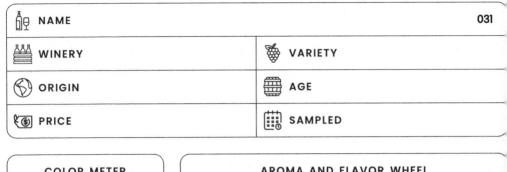

NAME	
WINERY	VARIETY
ORIGIN	AGE
PRICE	SAMPLED

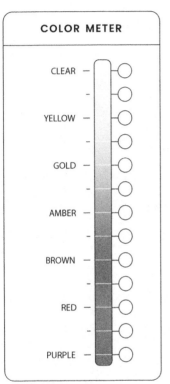

COLOR METER

CLEAR
—
YELLOW
—
GOLD
—
AMBER
—
BROWN
—
RED
—
PURPLE

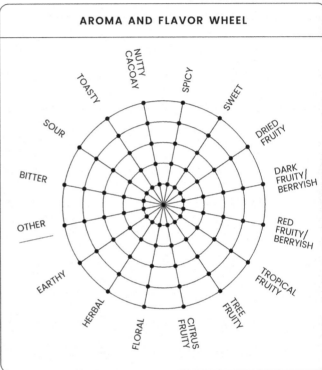

AROMA AND FLAVOR WHEEL

NUTTY CACOAY
TOASTY
SPICY
SWEET
SOUR
DRIED FRUITY
BITTER
DARK FRUITY/ BERRYISH
OTHER
RED FRUITY/ BERRYISH
EARTHY
TROPICAL FRUITY
HERBAL
TREE FRUITY
FLORAL
CITRUS FRUITY

NOTES AND RATING

APPEARANCE	☆☆☆☆☆
AROMA	☆☆☆☆☆
FLAVOR	☆☆☆☆☆
OVERALL RATING	☆☆☆☆☆

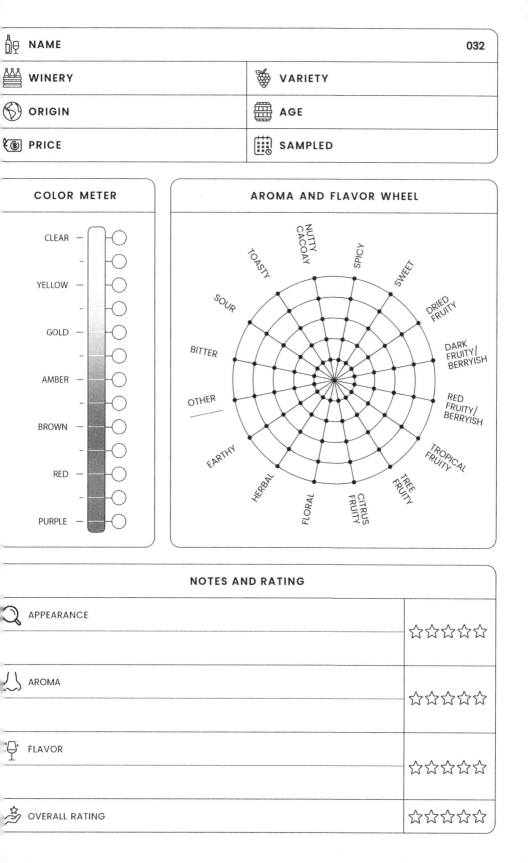

NAME

032

WINERY

VARIETY

ORIGIN

AGE

PRICE

SAMPLED

COLOR METER

CLEAR

—

YELLOW

—

GOLD

—

AMBER

—

BROWN

—

RED

—

PURPLE

AROMA AND FLAVOR WHEEL

NUTTY CACOAY
SPICY
TOASTY
SWEET
SOUR
DRIED FRUITY
BITTER
DARK FRUITY/ BERRYISH
OTHER
RED FRUITY/ BERRYISH
EARTHY
TROPICAL FRUITY
HERBAL
TREE FRUITY
FLORAL
CITRUS FRUITY

NOTES AND RATING

APPEARANCE

☆☆☆☆☆

AROMA

☆☆☆☆☆

FLAVOR

☆☆☆☆☆

OVERALL RATING

☆☆☆☆☆

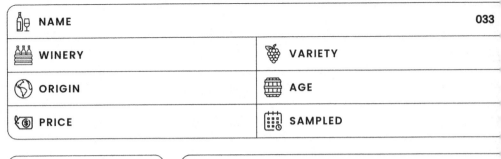

NAME	**033**

WINERY	**VARIETY**
ORIGIN	**AGE**
PRICE	**SAMPLED**

COLOR METER

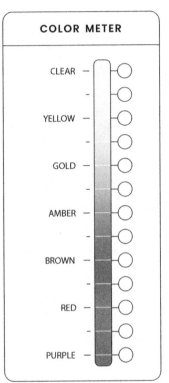

CLEAR

YELLOW

GOLD

AMBER

BROWN

RED

PURPLE

AROMA AND FLAVOR WHEEL

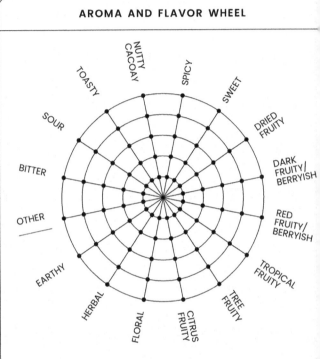

NUTTY CACOAY · SPICY · SWEET · DRIED FRUITY · DARK FRUITY/BERRYISH · RED FRUITY/BERRYISH · TROPICAL FRUITY · TREE FRUITY · CITRUS FRUITY · FLORAL · HERBAL · EARTHY · OTHER · BITTER · SOUR · TOASTY

NOTES AND RATING

APPEARANCE ☆☆☆☆☆

AROMA ☆☆☆☆☆

FLAVOR ☆☆☆☆☆

OVERALL RATING ☆☆☆☆☆

🍾 NAME		034
🍾 WINERY	🍇 VARIETY	
🌐 ORIGIN	🛢 AGE	
💲 PRICE	📅 SAMPLED	

COLOR METER

- CLEAR
- –
- YELLOW
- –
- GOLD
- –
- AMBER
- –
- BROWN
- –
- RED
- –
- PURPLE

AROMA AND FLAVOR WHEEL

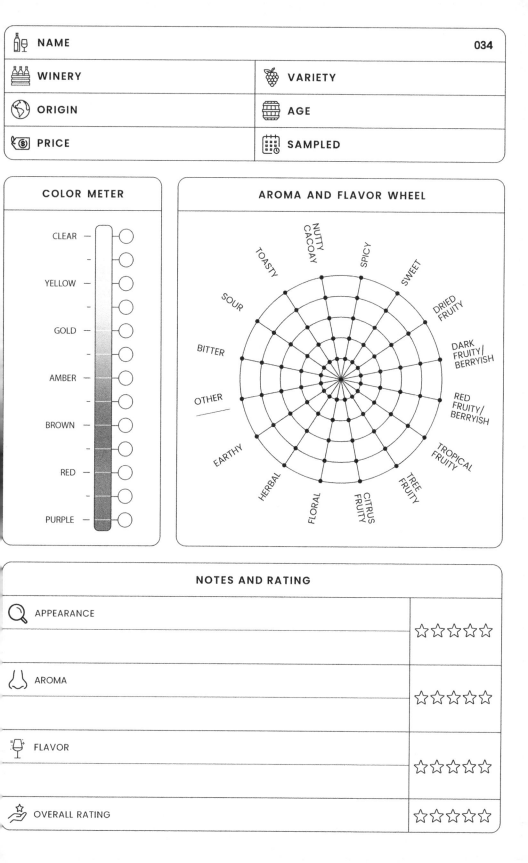

NUTTY CACOAY · SPICY · SWEET · DRIED FRUITY · DARK FRUITY/BERRYISH · RED FRUITY/BERRYISH · TROPICAL FRUITY · TREE FRUITY · CITRUS FRUITY · FLORAL · HERBAL · EARTHY · OTHER · BITTER · SOUR · TOASTY

NOTES AND RATING

🔍 APPEARANCE ☆☆☆☆☆

👃 AROMA ☆☆☆☆☆

🍷 FLAVOR ☆☆☆☆☆

🖐 OVERALL RATING ☆☆☆☆☆

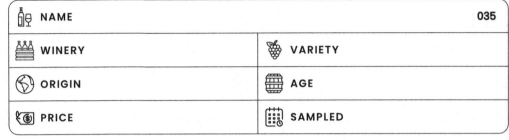

🍷 NAME		035
🍾 WINERY		🍇 VARIETY
🌐 ORIGIN		🛢️ AGE
💵 PRICE		📅 SAMPLED

COLOR METER

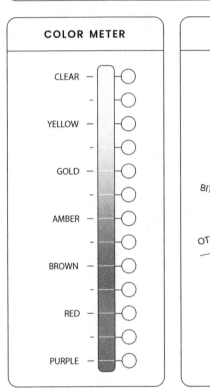

CLEAR —
–
YELLOW —
–
GOLD —
–
AMBER —
–
BROWN —
–
RED —
–
PURPLE —

AROMA AND FLAVOR WHEEL

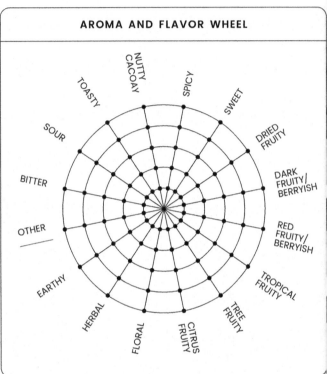

NUTTY CACOAY
SPICY
TOASTY
SWEET
SOUR
DRIED FRUITY
BITTER
DARK FRUITY/ BERRYISH
OTHER
RED FRUITY/ BERRYISH
EARTHY
TROPICAL FRUITY
HERBAL
TREE FRUITY
FLORAL
CITRUS FRUITY

NOTES AND RATING

🔍 APPEARANCE
☆☆☆☆☆

👃 AROMA
☆☆☆☆☆

🍷 FLAVOR
☆☆☆☆☆

🙌 OVERALL RATING
☆☆☆☆☆

🍾 **NAME**			**036**

🍺 **WINERY**	🍇 **VARIETY**	
🌍 **ORIGIN**	🛢 **AGE**	
💰 **PRICE**	📅 **SAMPLED**	

COLOR METER

- CLEAR
- —
- YELLOW
- —
- GOLD
- —
- AMBER
- —
- BROWN
- —
- RED
- —
- PURPLE

AROMA AND FLAVOR WHEEL

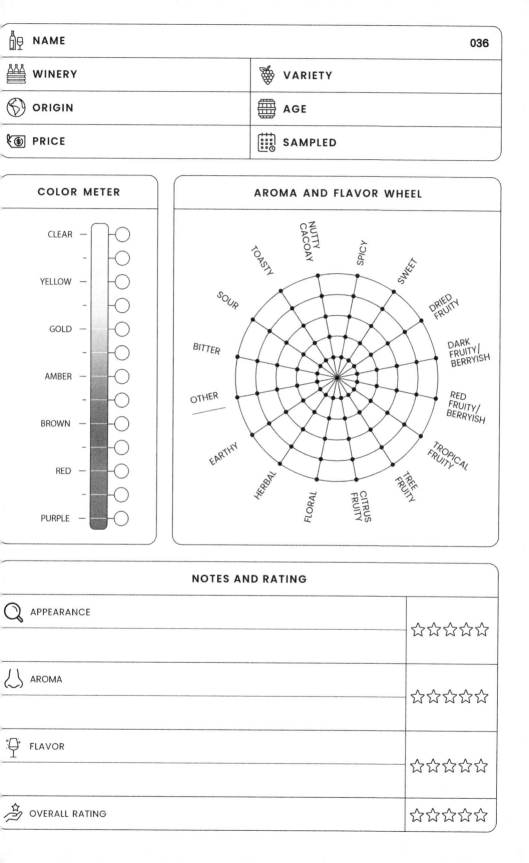

NUTTY CACOAY · TOASTY · SPICY · SOUR · SWEET · BITTER · DRIED FRUITY · OTHER · DARK FRUITY/BERRYISH · RED FRUITY/BERRYISH · EARTHY · TROPICAL FRUITY · HERBAL · TREE FRUITY · FLORAL · CITRUS FRUITY

NOTES AND RATING

🔍 APPEARANCE	☆☆☆☆☆
👃 AROMA	☆☆☆☆☆
🍷 FLAVOR	☆☆☆☆☆
🖐 OVERALL RATING	☆☆☆☆☆

NAME

WINERY	VARIETY
ORIGIN	AGE
PRICE	SAMPLED

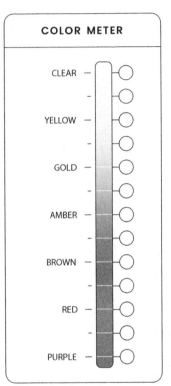

COLOR METER

- CLEAR
- –
- YELLOW
- –
- GOLD
- –
- AMBER
- –
- BROWN
- –
- RED
- –
- PURPLE

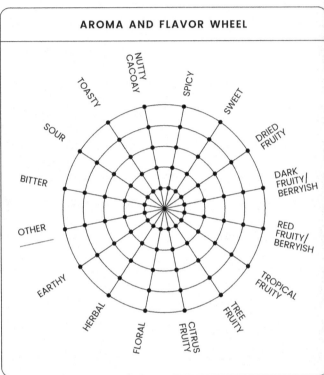

AROMA AND FLAVOR WHEEL

NUTTY CACOAY · SPICY · SWEET · DRIED FRUITY · DARK FRUITY/BERRYISH · RED FRUITY/BERRYISH · TROPICAL FRUITY · TREE FRUITY · CITRUS FRUITY · FLORAL · HERBAL · EARTHY · OTHER · BITTER · SOUR · TOASTY

NOTES AND RATING

APPEARANCE	☆☆☆☆☆
AROMA	☆☆☆☆☆
FLAVOR	☆☆☆☆☆
OVERALL RATING	☆☆☆☆☆

🍷 **NAME**		038
🍾 **WINERY**	🍇 **VARIETY**	
🌐 **ORIGIN**	🛢 **AGE**	
💲 **PRICE**	📅 **SAMPLED**	

COLOR METER

CLEAR —

—

YELLOW —

—

GOLD —

—

AMBER —

—

BROWN —

—

RED —

—

PURPLE —

AROMA AND FLAVOR WHEEL

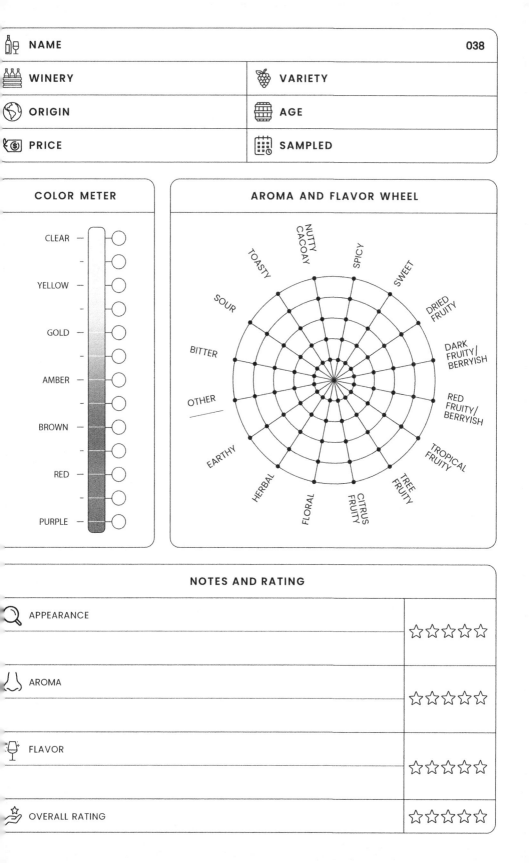

NUTTY
CACOAY
TOASTY
SPICY
SOUR
SWEET
BITTER
DRIED FRUITY
OTHER
DARK FRUITY/BERRYISH
EARTHY
RED FRUITY/BERRYISH
HERBAL
TROPICAL FRUITY
FLORAL
TREE FRUITY
CITRUS FRUITY

NOTES AND RATING

🔍 **APPEARANCE**

☆☆☆☆☆

👃 **AROMA**

☆☆☆☆☆

🍷 **FLAVOR**

☆☆☆☆☆

⭐ **OVERALL RATING**

☆☆☆☆☆

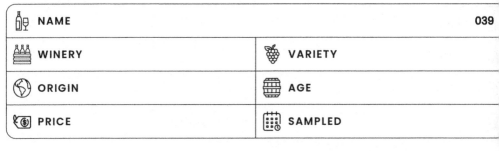

🍾 **NAME**	
🍶 **WINERY**	🍇 **VARIETY**
🌐 **ORIGIN**	🛢 **AGE**
💰 **PRICE**	📅 **SAMPLED**

COLOR METER

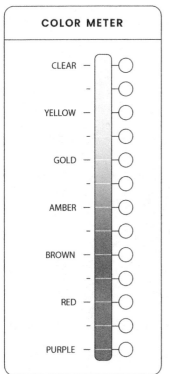

CLEAR
—
YELLOW
—
GOLD
—
AMBER
—
BROWN
—
RED
—
PURPLE

AROMA AND FLAVOR WHEEL

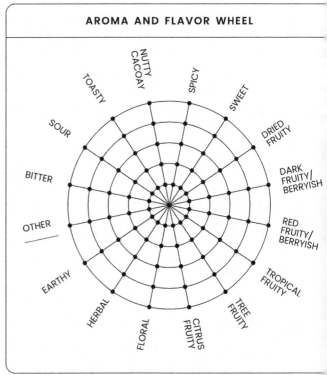

NUTTY CACOAY · SPICY · SWEET · DRIED FRUITY · DARK FRUITY/BERRYISH · RED FRUITY/BERRYISH · TROPICAL FRUITY · TREE FRUITY · CITRUS FRUITY · FLORAL · HERBAL · EARTHY · OTHER · BITTER · SOUR · TOASTY

NOTES AND RATING

🔍 **APPEARANCE**

☆☆☆☆☆

👃 **AROMA**

☆☆☆☆☆

🥂 **FLAVOR**

☆☆☆☆☆

🤲 **OVERALL RATING**

☆☆☆☆☆

🍾 NAME		040
🍱 WINERY	🍇 VARIETY	
🌍 ORIGIN	🛢 AGE	
💲 PRICE	📅 SAMPLED	

COLOR METER

CLEAR —
—
YELLOW —
—
GOLD —
—
AMBER —
—
BROWN —
—
RED —
—
PURPLE —

AROMA AND FLAVOR WHEEL

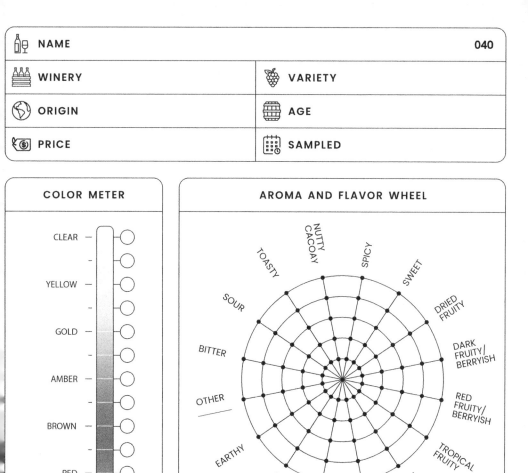

NUTTY CACOAY
TOASTY
SPICY
SWEET
SOUR
DRIED FRUITY
BITTER
DARK FRUITY/ BERRYISH
OTHER
RED FRUITY/ BERRYISH
EARTHY
TROPICAL FRUITY
HERBAL
TREE FRUITY
FLORAL
CITRUS FRUITY

NOTES AND RATING

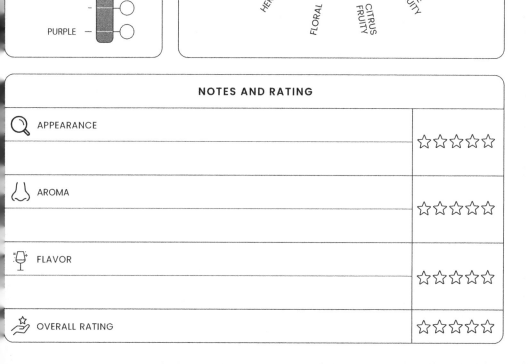

🔍 APPEARANCE
☆☆☆☆☆

👃 AROMA
☆☆☆☆☆

🍷 FLAVOR
☆☆☆☆☆

🖐 OVERALL RATING
☆☆☆☆☆

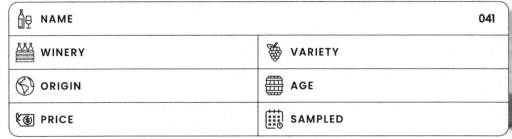

🍾 **NAME**		041
🍾 **WINERY**	🍇 **VARIETY**	
🌐 **ORIGIN**	🛢 **AGE**	
💵 **PRICE**	📅 **SAMPLED**	

COLOR METER

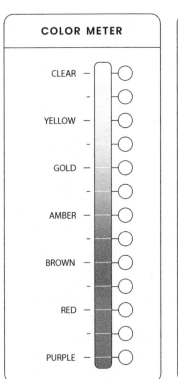

CLEAR —
-
YELLOW —
-
GOLD —
-
AMBER —
-
BROWN —
-
RED —
-
PURPLE —

AROMA AND FLAVOR WHEEL

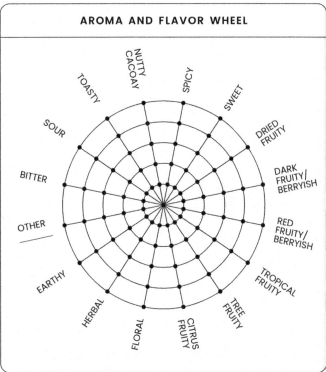

NUTTY CACOAY
TOASTY
SPICY
SOUR
SWEET
BITTER
DRIED FRUITY
OTHER
DARK FRUITY/ BERRYISH
EARTHY
RED FRUITY/ BERRYISH
HERBAL
TROPICAL FRUITY
FLORAL
TREE FRUITY
CITRUS FRUITY

NOTES AND RATING

🔍 APPEARANCE	☆☆☆☆☆
👃 AROMA	☆☆☆☆☆
🍷 FLAVOR	☆☆☆☆☆
🖐 OVERALL RATING	☆☆☆☆☆

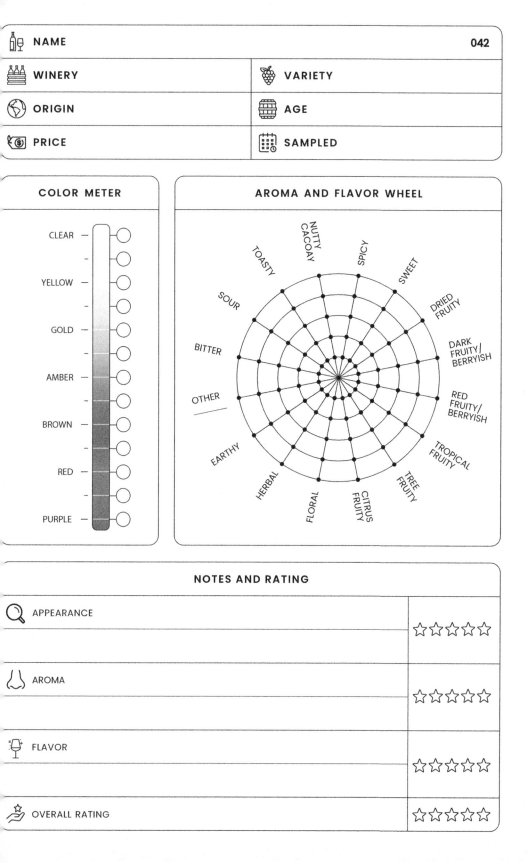

NAME

042

WINERY	**VARIETY**
ORIGIN	**AGE**
PRICE	**SAMPLED**

COLOR METER

- CLEAR
- —
- YELLOW
- —
- GOLD
- —
- AMBER
- —
- BROWN
- —
- RED
- —
- PURPLE

AROMA AND FLAVOR WHEEL

NUTTY CACOAY
SPICY
TOASTY
SWEET
SOUR
DRIED FRUITY
BITTER
DARK FRUITY / BERRYISH
OTHER
RED FRUITY / BERRYISH
EARTHY
TROPICAL FRUITY
HERBAL
TREE FRUITY
FLORAL
CITRUS FRUITY

NOTES AND RATING

APPEARANCE ☆☆☆☆☆

AROMA ☆☆☆☆☆

FLAVOR ☆☆☆☆☆

OVERALL RATING ☆☆☆☆☆

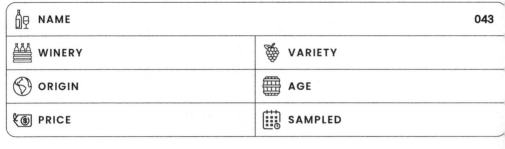

🍾 NAME		043
🍾 WINERY	🍇 VARIETY	
🌍 ORIGIN	🛢 AGE	
💵 PRICE	📅 SAMPLED	

COLOR METER

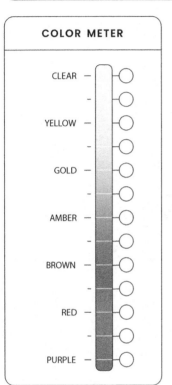

CLEAR —
—
YELLOW —
—
GOLD —
—
AMBER —
—
BROWN —
—
RED —
—
PURPLE —

AROMA AND FLAVOR WHEEL

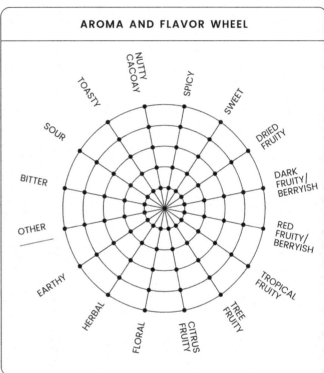

NUTTY CACOAY
TOASTY
SPICY
SOUR
SWEET
BITTER
DRIED FRUITY
DARK FRUITY/ BERRYISH
OTHER
RED FRUITY/ BERRYISH
EARTHY
TROPICAL FRUITY
HERBAL
TREE FRUITY
FLORAL
CITRUS FRUITY

NOTES AND RATING

🔍 APPEARANCE	☆☆☆☆☆
👃 AROMA	☆☆☆☆☆
🍷 FLAVOR	☆☆☆☆☆
🖐 OVERALL RATING	☆☆☆☆☆

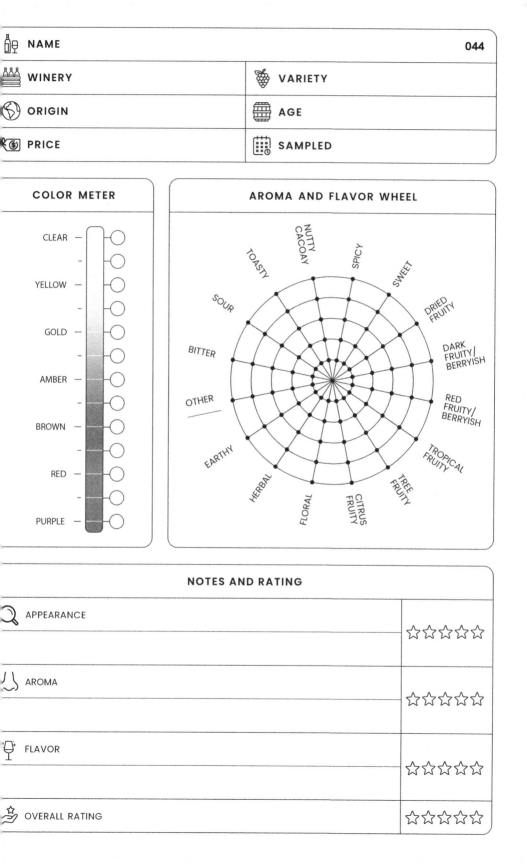

NAME

WINERY

VARIETY

ORIGIN

AGE

PRICE

SAMPLED

COLOR METER

CLEAR —

–

YELLOW —

–

GOLD —

–

AMBER —

–

BROWN —

–

RED —

–

PURPLE —

AROMA AND FLAVOR WHEEL

NUTTY CACOAY

TOASTY

SPICY

SWEET

SOUR

DRIED FRUITY

BITTER

DARK FRUITY/ BERRYISH

OTHER

RED FRUITY/ BERRYISH

EARTHY

TROPICAL FRUITY

HERBAL

TREE FRUITY

FLORAL

CITRUS FRUITY

NOTES AND RATING

APPEARANCE

☆☆☆☆☆

AROMA

☆☆☆☆☆

FLAVOR

☆☆☆☆☆

OVERALL RATING

☆☆☆☆☆

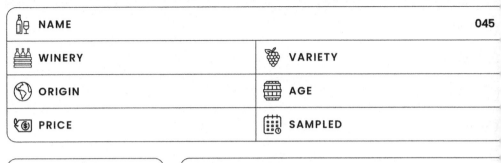

🍾 NAME	045

🍻 WINERY	🍇 VARIETY
🌐 ORIGIN	🛢 AGE
💰 PRICE	📅 SAMPLED

COLOR METER

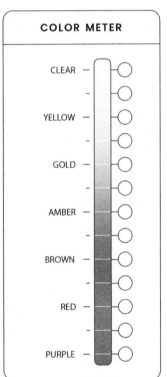

CLEAR —
—
YELLOW —
—
GOLD —
—
AMBER —
—
BROWN —
—
RED —
—
PURPLE —

AROMA AND FLAVOR WHEEL

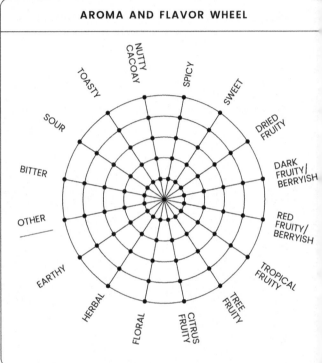

NUTTY CACOAY
TOASTY
SPICY
SWEET
SOUR
DRIED FRUITY
BITTER
DARK FRUITY/ BERRYISH
OTHER
RED FRUITY/ BERRYISH
EARTHY
TROPICAL FRUITY
HERBAL
TREE FRUITY
FLORAL
CITRUS FRUITY

NOTES AND RATING

🔍 APPEARANCE	☆☆☆☆☆

👃 AROMA	☆☆☆☆☆

🍷 FLAVOR	☆☆☆☆☆

🖐 OVERALL RATING	☆☆☆☆☆

NAME		046
WINERY	VARIETY	
ORIGIN	AGE	
PRICE	SAMPLED	

COLOR METER

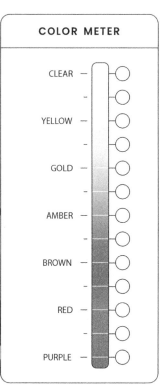

CLEAR

YELLOW

GOLD

AMBER

BROWN

RED

PURPLE

AROMA AND FLAVOR WHEEL

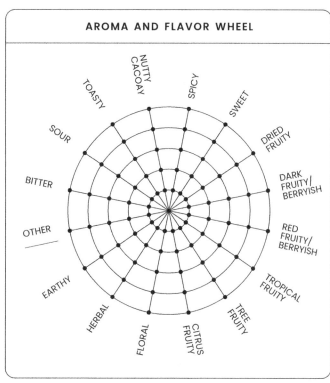

NUTTY CACOAY · SPICY · SWEET · DRIED FRUITY · DARK FRUITY/BERRYISH · RED FRUITY/BERRYISH · TROPICAL FRUITY · TREE FRUITY · CITRUS FRUITY · FLORAL · HERBAL · EARTHY · OTHER · BITTER · SOUR · TOASTY

NOTES AND RATING

APPEARANCE	☆☆☆☆☆
AROMA	☆☆☆☆☆
FLAVOR	☆☆☆☆☆
OVERALL RATING	☆☆☆☆☆

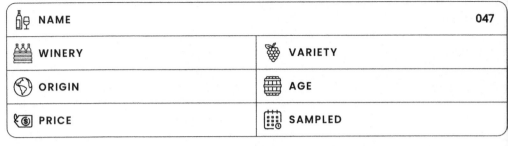

🍾 NAME	047

🍷 WINERY	🍇 VARIETY
🌍 ORIGIN	🛢 AGE
💵 PRICE	📅 SAMPLED

COLOR METER

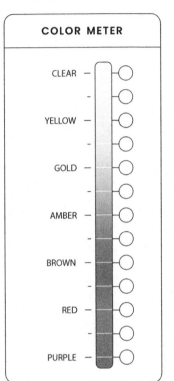

CLEAR —
-
YELLOW —
-
GOLD —
-
AMBER —
-
BROWN —
-
RED —
-
PURPLE —

AROMA AND FLAVOR WHEEL

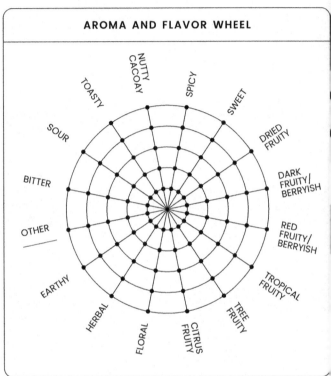

NUTTY CACAOY
SPICY
TOASTY
SWEET
SOUR
DRIED FRUITY
BITTER
DARK FRUITY/ BERRYISH
OTHER
RED FRUITY/ BERRYISH
EARTHY
TROPICAL FRUITY
HERBAL
TREE FRUITY
FLORAL
CITRUS FRUITY

NOTES AND RATING

🔍 APPEARANCE	☆☆☆☆☆
👃 AROMA	☆☆☆☆☆
🍷 FLAVOR	☆☆☆☆☆
🖐 OVERALL RATING	☆☆☆☆☆

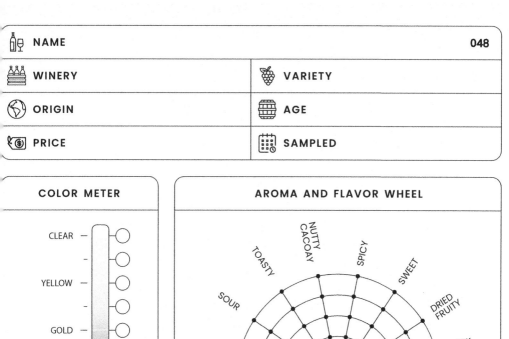

NAME		048
WINERY	VARIETY	
ORIGIN	AGE	
PRICE	SAMPLED	

COLOR METER

CLEAR —
—
YELLOW —
—
GOLD —
—
AMBER —
—
BROWN —
—
RED —
—
PURPLE —

AROMA AND FLAVOR WHEEL

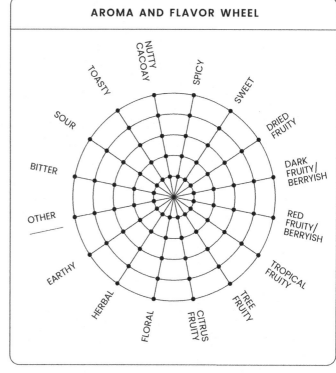

NUTTY CACOAY
TOASTY
SPICY
SWEET
SOUR
DRIED FRUITY
BITTER
DARK FRUITY / BERRYISH
OTHER
RED FRUITY / BERRYISH
EARTHY
TROPICAL FRUITY
HERBAL
TREE FRUITY
FLORAL
CITRUS FRUITY

NOTES AND RATING

APPEARANCE ☆☆☆☆☆

AROMA ☆☆☆☆☆

FLAVOR ☆☆☆☆☆

OVERALL RATING ☆☆☆☆☆

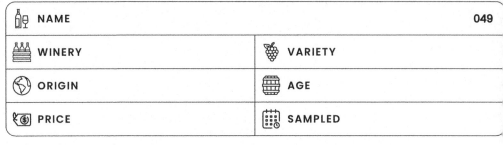

🍷 NAME		049
🍾 WINERY	🍇 VARIETY	
🌍 ORIGIN	🛢 AGE	
💵 PRICE	📅 SAMPLED	

COLOR METER

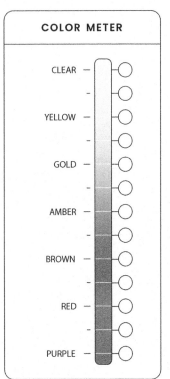

CLEAR —
–
YELLOW —
–
GOLD —
–
AMBER —
–
BROWN —
–
RED —
–
PURPLE —

AROMA AND FLAVOR WHEEL

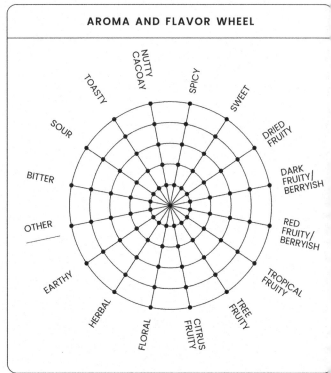

NUTTY CACOAY
SPICY
SWEET
DRIED FRUITY
DARK FRUITY/BERRYISH
RED FRUITY/BERRYISH
TROPICAL FRUITY
TREE FRUITY
CITRUS FRUITY
FLORAL
HERBAL
EARTHY
OTHER
BITTER
SOUR
TOASTY

NOTES AND RATING

🔍 APPEARANCE	☆☆☆☆☆

👃 AROMA	☆☆☆☆☆

🥂 FLAVOR	☆☆☆☆☆

🏆 OVERALL RATING	☆☆☆☆☆

NAME

WINERY	VARIETY
ORIGIN	AGE
PRICE	SAMPLED

COLOR METER

CLEAR —
–
YELLOW —
–
GOLD —
–
AMBER —
–
BROWN —
–
RED —
–
PURPLE —

AROMA AND FLAVOR WHEEL

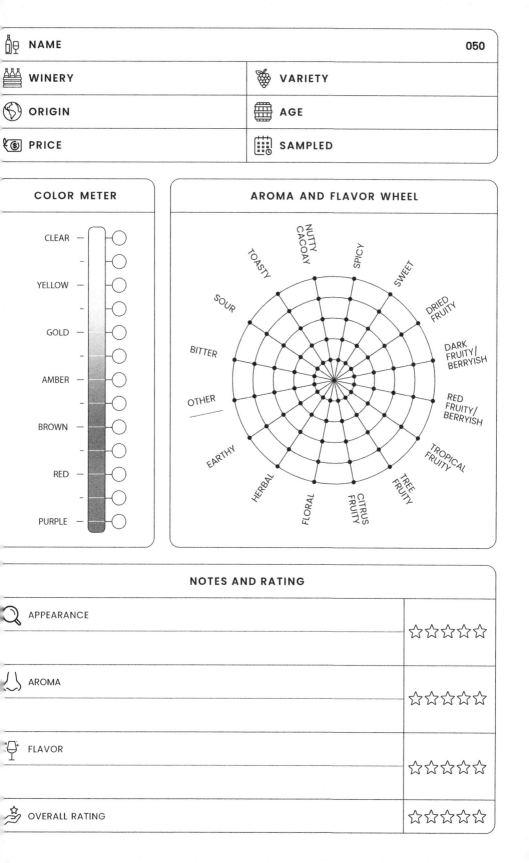

NUTTY CACOAY
SPICY
SWEET
TOASTY
DRIED FRUITY
SOUR
DARK FRUITY/ BERRYISH
BITTER
OTHER
RED FRUITY/ BERRYISH
EARTHY
TROPICAL FRUITY
HERBAL
TREE FRUITY
FLORAL
CITRUS FRUITY

NOTES AND RATING

APPEARANCE
☆☆☆☆☆

AROMA
☆☆☆☆☆

FLAVOR
☆☆☆☆☆

OVERALL RATING
☆☆☆☆☆

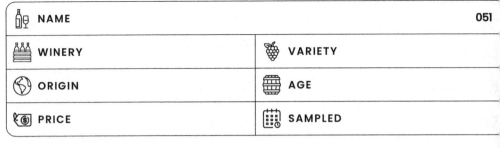

 🍾 NAME	051

🍷 WINERY	🍇 VARIETY
🌐 ORIGIN	🛢 AGE
💵 PRICE	📅 SAMPLED

COLOR METER

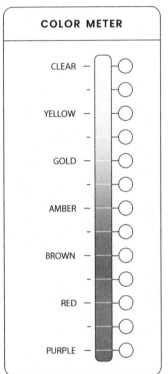

CLEAR —
—
YELLOW —
—
GOLD —
—
AMBER —
—
BROWN —
—
RED —
—
PURPLE —

AROMA AND FLAVOR WHEEL

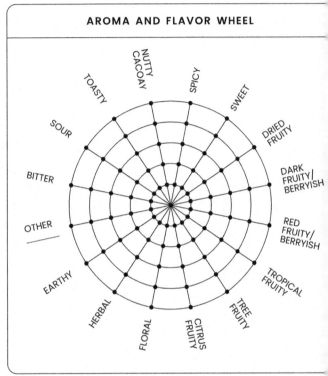

NUTTY CACOAY · SPICY · SWEET · DRIED FRUITY · DARK FRUITY/BERRYISH · RED FRUITY/BERRYISH · TROPICAL FRUITY · TREE FRUITY · CITRUS FRUITY · FLORAL · HERBAL · EARTHY · OTHER · BITTER · SOUR · TOASTY

NOTES AND RATING

🔍 APPEARANCE	☆☆☆☆☆
👃 AROMA	☆☆☆☆☆
🍷 FLAVOR	☆☆☆☆☆
🖐 OVERALL RATING	☆☆☆☆☆

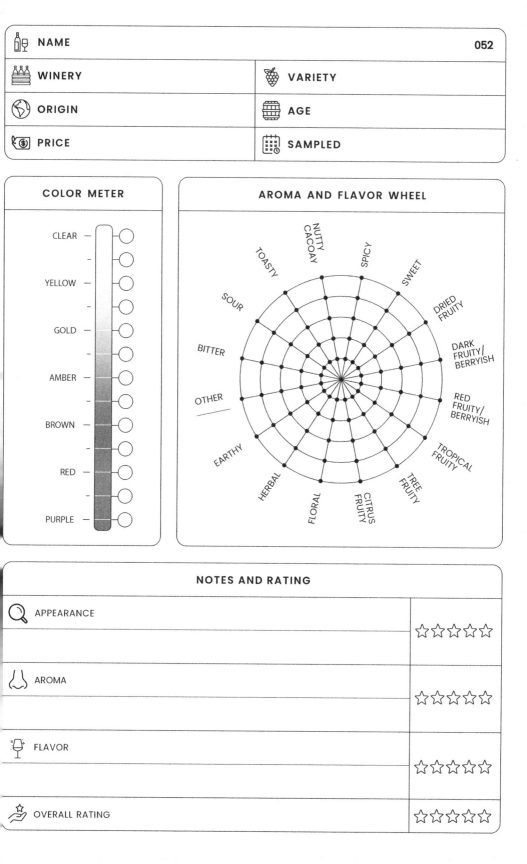 NAME		052
WINERY	VARIETY	
ORIGIN	AGE	
PRICE	SAMPLED	

COLOR METER

- CLEAR —
- —
- YELLOW —
- —
- GOLD —
- —
- AMBER —
- —
- BROWN —
- —
- RED —
- —
- PURPLE —

AROMA AND FLAVOR WHEEL

NUTTY CACOAY · SPICY · SWEET · TOASTY · DRIED FRUITY · SOUR · DARK FRUITY/BERRYISH · BITTER · RED FRUITY/BERRYISH · OTHER · TROPICAL FRUITY · EARTHY · TREE FRUITY · HERBAL · CITRUS FRUITY · FLORAL

NOTES AND RATING

APPEARANCE	☆☆☆☆☆
AROMA	☆☆☆☆☆
FLAVOR	☆☆☆☆☆
OVERALL RATING	☆☆☆☆☆

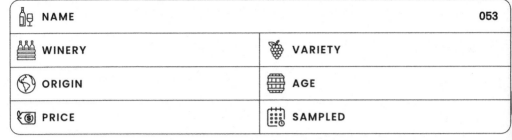

🍾 NAME	053

🍻 WINERY	🍇 VARIETY
🌍 ORIGIN	🛢️ AGE
💸 PRICE	📅 SAMPLED

COLOR METER

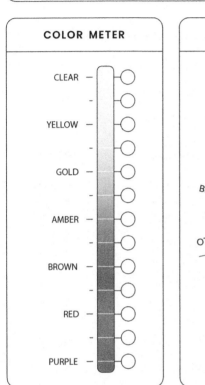

CLEAR

YELLOW

GOLD

AMBER

BROWN

RED

PURPLE

AROMA AND FLAVOR WHEEL

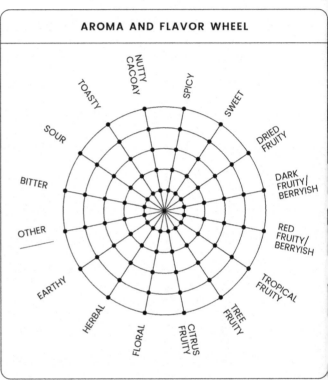

NUTTY CACOAY · SPICY · SWEET · DRIED FRUITY · DARK FRUITY/BERRYISH · RED FRUITY/BERRYISH · TROPICAL FRUITY · TREE FRUITY · CITRUS FRUITY · FLORAL · HERBAL · EARTHY · OTHER · BITTER · SOUR · TOASTY

NOTES AND RATING

🔍 APPEARANCE	☆☆☆☆☆

👃 AROMA	☆☆☆☆☆

🍷 FLAVOR	☆☆☆☆☆

🏆 OVERALL RATING	☆☆☆☆☆

NAME

054

🍾 **NAME**		**054**
🍶 **WINERY**	🍇 **VARIETY**	
🌍 **ORIGIN**	🛢 **AGE**	
💵 **PRICE**	📅 **SAMPLED**	

COLOR METER

- CLEAR —
- —
- YELLOW —
- —
- GOLD —
- —
- AMBER —
- —
- BROWN —
- —
- RED —
- —
- PURPLE —

AROMA AND FLAVOR WHEEL

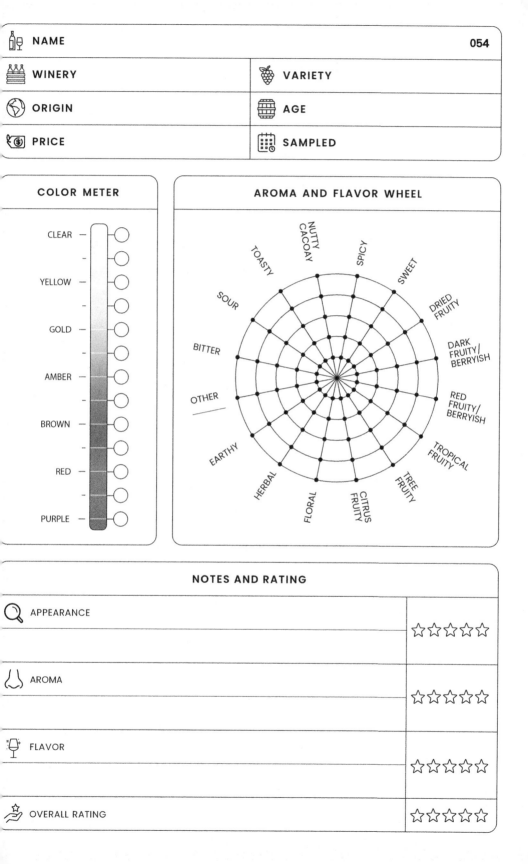

NUTTY CACOAY · SPICY · TOASTY · SWEET · SOUR · DRIED FRUITY · BITTER · DARK FRUITY/BERRYISH · OTHER · RED FRUITY/BERRYISH · EARTHY · TROPICAL FRUITY · HERBAL · TREE FRUITY · FLORAL · CITRUS FRUITY

NOTES AND RATING

🔍 **APPEARANCE**
☆☆☆☆☆

👃 **AROMA**
☆☆☆☆☆

🍷 **FLAVOR**
☆☆☆☆☆

🖐 **OVERALL RATING**
☆☆☆☆☆

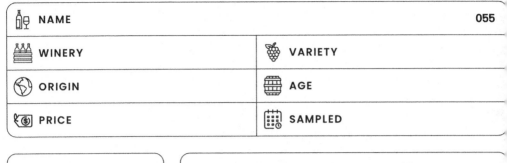

🍾 NAME	055

🍾 WINERY	🍇 VARIETY
🌍 ORIGIN	🛢 AGE
💵 PRICE	📅 SAMPLED

COLOR METER

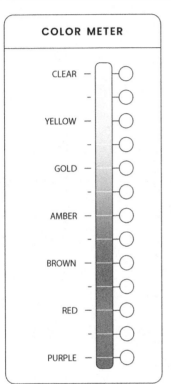

CLEAR —
—
YELLOW —
—
GOLD —
—
AMBER —
—
BROWN —
—
RED —
—
PURPLE —

AROMA AND FLAVOR WHEEL

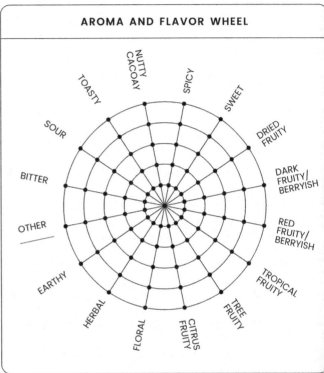

NUTTY CACOAY
TOASTY
SPICY
SOUR
SWEET
BITTER
DRIED FRUITY
DARK FRUITY/ BERRYISH
OTHER
RED FRUITY/ BERRYISH
EARTHY
TROPICAL FRUITY
HERBAL
TREE FRUITY
FLORAL
CITRUS FRUITY

NOTES AND RATING

🔍 APPEARANCE	☆☆☆☆☆
👃 AROMA	☆☆☆☆☆
🍷 FLAVOR	☆☆☆☆☆
🤲 OVERALL RATING	☆☆☆☆☆

NAME

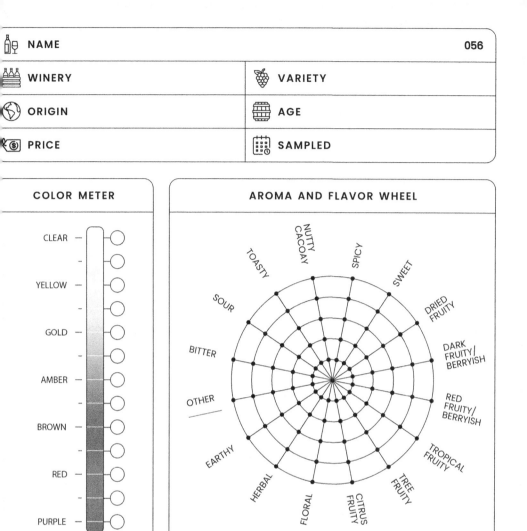

056

WINERY	VARIETY
ORIGIN	AGE
PRICE	SAMPLED

COLOR METER

CLEAR —

–

YELLOW —

–

GOLD —

–

AMBER —

–

BROWN —

–

RED —

–

PURPLE —

AROMA AND FLAVOR WHEEL

NUTTY CACOAY

TOASTY

SPICY

SOUR

SWEET

BITTER

DRIED FRUITY

OTHER

DARK FRUITY/ BERRYISH

EARTHY

RED FRUITY/ BERRYISH

HERBAL

TROPICAL FRUITY

FLORAL

CITRUS FRUITY

TREE FRUITY

NOTES AND RATING

APPEARANCE

☆☆☆☆☆

AROMA

☆☆☆☆☆

FLAVOR

☆☆☆☆☆

OVERALL RATING

☆☆☆☆☆

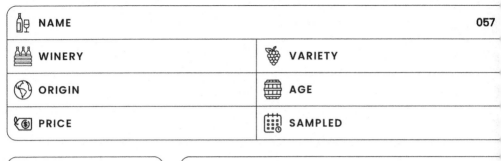

🍾 **NAME**			
🍾 **WINERY**		🍇 **VARIETY**	
🌍 **ORIGIN**		🛢️ **AGE**	
💵 **PRICE**		📅 **SAMPLED**	

COLOR METER

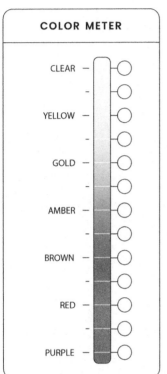

CLEAR —
—
YELLOW —
—
GOLD —
—
AMBER —
—
BROWN —
—
RED —
—
PURPLE —

AROMA AND FLAVOR WHEEL

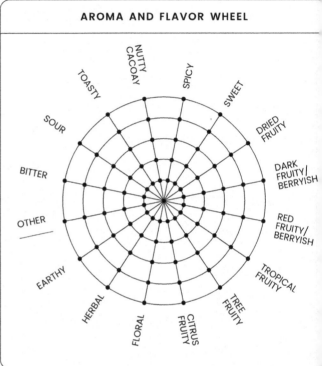

NUTTY CACOAY · SPICY · SWEET · DRIED FRUITY · DARK FRUITY/BERRYISH · RED FRUITY/BERRYISH · TROPICAL FRUITY · TREE FRUITY · CITRUS FRUITY · FLORAL · HERBAL · EARTHY · OTHER · BITTER · SOUR · TOASTY

NOTES AND RATING

🔍 **APPEARANCE**

☆☆☆☆☆

👃 **AROMA**

☆☆☆☆☆

🍷 **FLAVOR**

☆☆☆☆☆

🖐️ **OVERALL RATING**

☆☆☆☆☆

NAME	058
WINERY	VARIETY
ORIGIN	AGE
PRICE	SAMPLED

COLOR METER

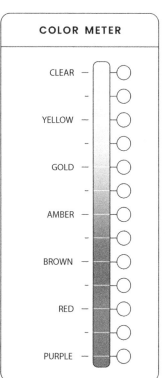

- CLEAR
- YELLOW
- GOLD
- AMBER
- BROWN
- RED
- PURPLE

AROMA AND FLAVOR WHEEL

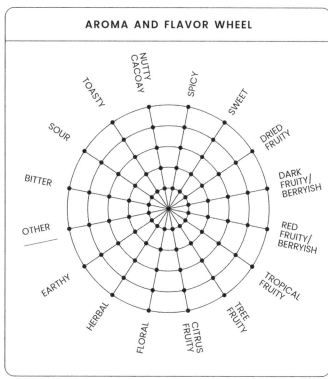

NUTTY CACOAY · SPICY · SWEET · DRIED FRUITY · DARK FRUITY/BERRYISH · RED FRUITY/BERRYISH · TROPICAL FRUITY · TREE FRUITY · CITRUS FRUITY · FLORAL · HERBAL · EARTHY · OTHER · BITTER · SOUR · TOASTY

NOTES AND RATING

Q APPEARANCE	☆☆☆☆☆
AROMA	☆☆☆☆☆
FLAVOR	☆☆☆☆☆
OVERALL RATING	☆☆☆☆☆

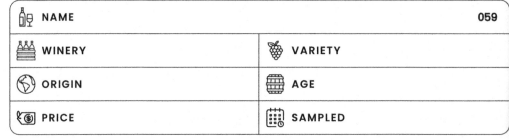

🍾 NAME	059
🍺 WINERY	🍇 VARIETY
🌍 ORIGIN	🛢️ AGE
💰 PRICE	📅 SAMPLED

COLOR METER

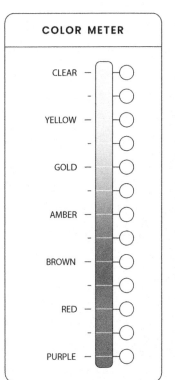

CLEAR —
–
YELLOW —
–
GOLD —
–
AMBER —
–
BROWN —
–
RED —
–
PURPLE —

AROMA AND FLAVOR WHEEL

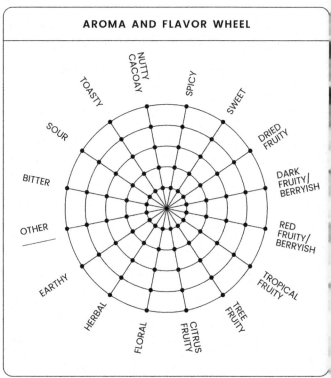

NUTTY CACOAY · SPICY · SWEET · DRIED FRUITY · DARK FRUITY / BERRYISH · RED FRUITY / BERRYISH · TROPICAL FRUITY · TREE FRUITY · CITRUS FRUITY · FLORAL · HERBAL · EARTHY · OTHER · BITTER · SOUR · TOASTY

NOTES AND RATING

🔍 APPEARANCE	☆☆☆☆☆
👃 AROMA	☆☆☆☆☆
🍷 FLAVOR	☆☆☆☆☆
🙌 OVERALL RATING	☆☆☆☆☆

🍾 **NAME**		060
🍾 **WINERY**	🐝 **VARIETY**	
🌐 **ORIGIN**	🛢 **AGE**	
💵 **PRICE**	📆 **SAMPLED**	

COLOR METER

- CLEAR
- –
- YELLOW
- –
- GOLD
- –
- AMBER
- –
- BROWN
- –
- RED
- –
- PURPLE

AROMA AND FLAVOR WHEEL

NUTTY CACOAY · TOASTY · SPICY · SWEET · SOUR · DRIED FRUITY · BITTER · DARK FRUITY/BERRYISH · OTHER · RED FRUITY/BERRYISH · EARTHY · TROPICAL FRUITY · HERBAL · TREE FRUITY · FLORAL · CITRUS FRUITY

NOTES AND RATING

🔍 **APPEARANCE** ☆☆☆☆☆

👃 **AROMA** ☆☆☆☆☆

🍷 **FLAVOR** ☆☆☆☆☆

✋ **OVERALL RATING** ☆☆☆☆☆

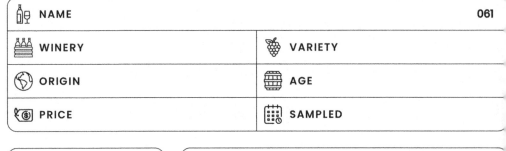

NAME

WINERY	**VARIETY**
ORIGIN	**AGE**
PRICE	**SAMPLED**

COLOR METER

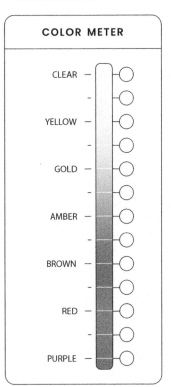

CLEAR
YELLOW
GOLD
AMBER
BROWN
RED
PURPLE

AROMA AND FLAVOR WHEEL

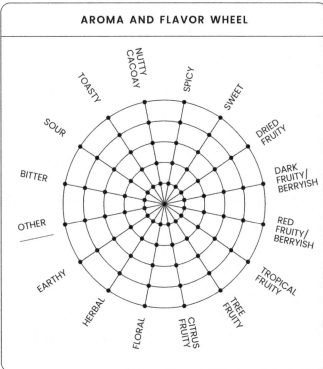

NUTTY CACOAY · SPICY · SWEET · DRIED FRUITY · DARK FRUITY/BERRYISH · RED FRUITY/BERRYISH · TROPICAL FRUITY · TREE FRUITY · CITRUS FRUITY · FLORAL · HERBAL · EARTHY · OTHER · BITTER · SOUR · TOASTY

NOTES AND RATING

APPEARANCE

☆☆☆☆☆

AROMA

☆☆☆☆☆

FLAVOR

☆☆☆☆☆

OVERALL RATING

☆☆☆☆☆

NAME

WINERY

VARIETY

ORIGIN

AGE

PRICE

SAMPLED

COLOR METER

CLEAR —
—
YELLOW —
—
GOLD —
—
AMBER —
—
BROWN —
—
RED —
—
PURPLE —

AROMA AND FLAVOR WHEEL

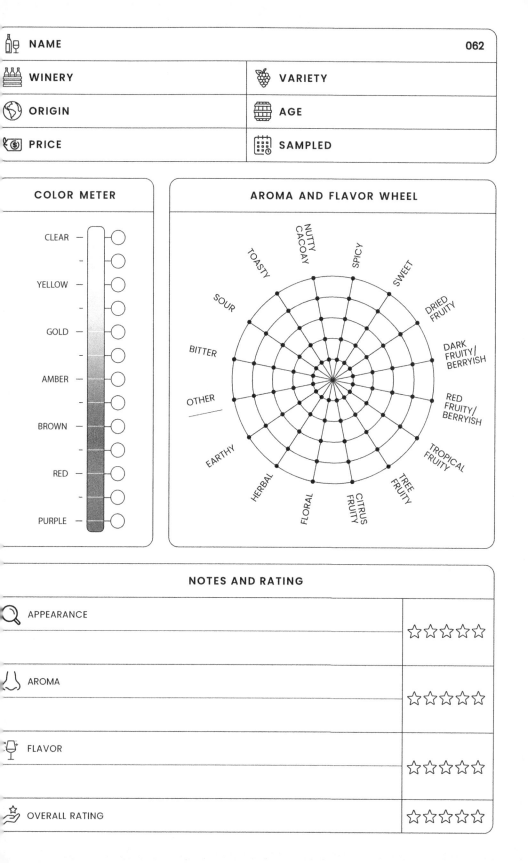

NUTTY CACOAY
TOASTY
SPICY
SOUR
SWEET
BITTER
DRIED FRUITY
OTHER
DARK FRUITY/ BERRYISH
EARTHY
RED FRUITY/ BERRYISH
HERBAL
TROPICAL FRUITY
FLORAL
TREE FRUITY
CITRUS FRUITY

NOTES AND RATING

APPEARANCE
☆☆☆☆☆

AROMA
☆☆☆☆☆

FLAVOR
☆☆☆☆☆

OVERALL RATING
☆☆☆☆☆

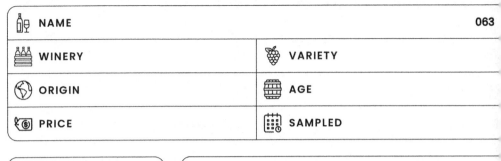

NAME	
WINERY	VARIETY
ORIGIN	AGE
PRICE	SAMPLED

COLOR METER

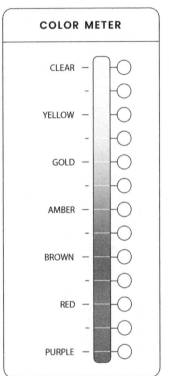

CLEAR

YELLOW

GOLD

AMBER

BROWN

RED

PURPLE

AROMA AND FLAVOR WHEEL

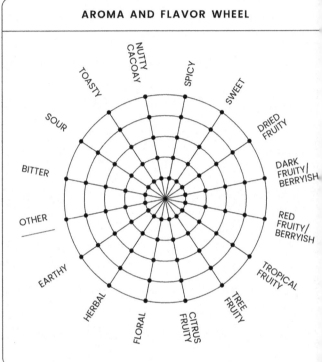

NUTTY CACOAY

SPICY

TOASTY

SWEET

SOUR

DRIED FRUITY

BITTER

DARK FRUITY/ BERRYISH

OTHER

RED FRUITY/ BERRYISH

EARTHY

TROPICAL FRUITY

HERBAL

TREE FRUITY

FLORAL

CITRUS FRUITY

NOTES AND RATING

APPEARANCE

☆☆☆☆☆

AROMA

☆☆☆☆☆

FLAVOR

☆☆☆☆☆

OVERALL RATING

☆☆☆☆☆

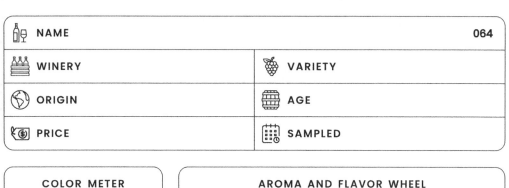

  NAME	064
WINERY	VARIETY
ORIGIN	AGE
PRICE	SAMPLED

COLOR METER

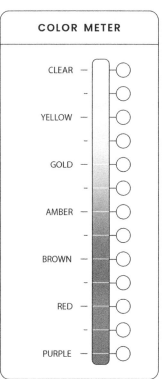

CLEAR

YELLOW

GOLD

AMBER

BROWN

RED

PURPLE

AROMA AND FLAVOR WHEEL

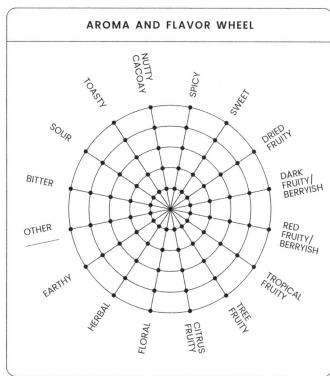

NUTTY CACOAY
TOASTY
SPICY
SWEET
SOUR
DRIED FRUITY
BITTER
DARK FRUITY/ BERRYISH
OTHER
RED FRUITY/ BERRYISH
EARTHY
TROPICAL FRUITY
HERBAL
TREE FRUITY
FLORAL
CITRUS FRUITY

NOTES AND RATING

🔍 APPEARANCE	☆☆☆☆☆
👃 AROMA	☆☆☆☆☆
🍷 FLAVOR	☆☆☆☆☆
🤲 OVERALL RATING	☆☆☆☆☆

🍾 NAME	065
🍻 WINERY	🍇 VARIETY
🌐 ORIGIN	🛢 AGE
💰 PRICE	📅 SAMPLED

COLOR METER

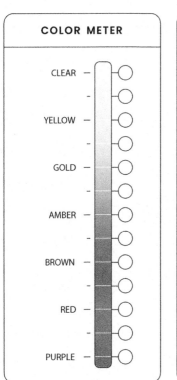

CLEAR —

YELLOW —

GOLD —

AMBER —

BROWN —

RED —

PURPLE —

AROMA AND FLAVOR WHEEL

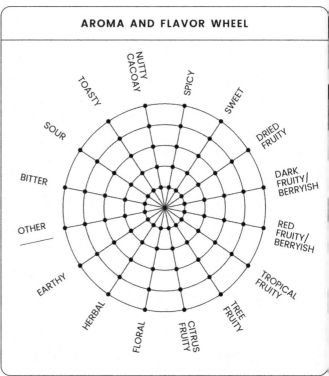

NUTTY CACOAY
SPICY
TOASTY
SWEET
SOUR
DRIED FRUITY
BITTER
DARK FRUITY/ BERRYISH
OTHER
RED FRUITY/ BERRYISH
EARTHY
TROPICAL FRUITY
HERBAL
TREE FRUITY
FLORAL
CITRUS FRUITY

NOTES AND RATING

🔍 APPEARANCE	☆☆☆☆☆
👃 AROMA	☆☆☆☆☆
🍷 FLAVOR	☆☆☆☆☆
🖐 OVERALL RATING	☆☆☆☆☆

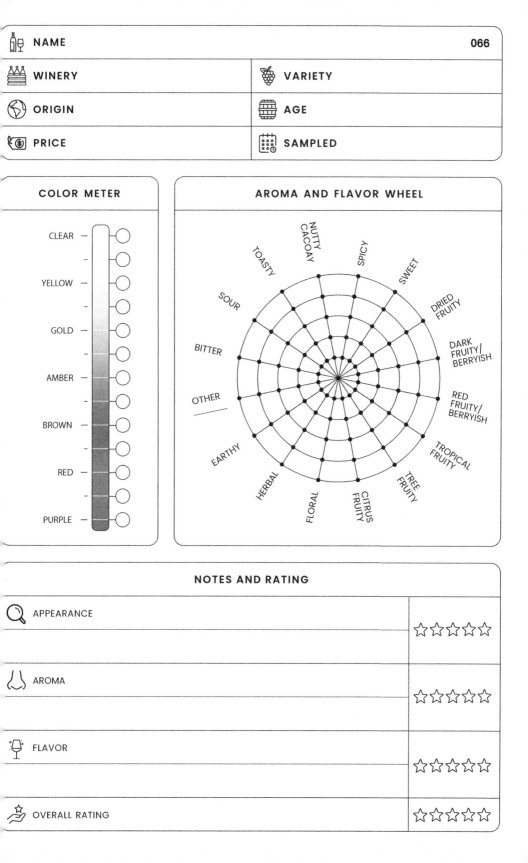

🍾 **NAME**		**066**
🍶 **WINERY**	🍇 **VARIETY**	
🌐 **ORIGIN**	🛢 **AGE**	
💵 **PRICE**	📅 **SAMPLED**	

COLOR METER

- CLEAR
- –
- YELLOW
- –
- GOLD
- –
- AMBER
- –
- BROWN
- –
- RED
- –
- PURPLE

AROMA AND FLAVOR WHEEL

NUTTY CACOAY
TOASTY
SPICY
SOUR
SWEET
BITTER
DRIED FRUITY
OTHER
DARK FRUITY/ BERRYISH
RED FRUITY/ BERRYISH
EARTHY
TROPICAL FRUITY
HERBAL
TREE FRUITY
FLORAL
CITRUS FRUITY

NOTES AND RATING

🔍 **APPEARANCE**

☆☆☆☆☆

👃 **AROMA**

☆☆☆☆☆

🍷 **FLAVOR**

☆☆☆☆☆

✋ **OVERALL RATING**

☆☆☆☆☆

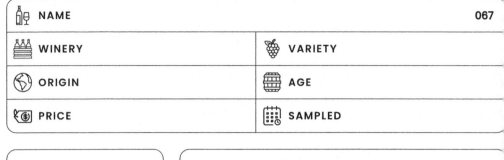

NAME			
WINERY		VARIETY	
ORIGIN		AGE	
PRICE		SAMPLED	

COLOR METER

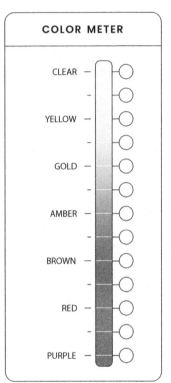

CLEAR
—
YELLOW
—
GOLD
—
AMBER
—
BROWN
—
RED
—
PURPLE

AROMA AND FLAVOR WHEEL

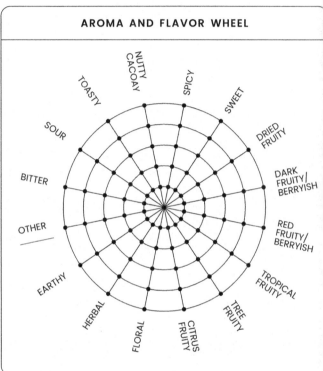

NUTTY CACOAY · SPICY · SWEET · DRIED FRUITY · DARK FRUITY/BERRYISH · RED FRUITY/BERRYISH · TROPICAL FRUITY · TREE FRUITY · CITRUS FRUITY · FLORAL · HERBAL · EARTHY · OTHER · BITTER · SOUR · TOASTY

NOTES AND RATING

APPEARANCE
☆☆☆☆☆

AROMA
☆☆☆☆☆

FLAVOR
☆☆☆☆☆

OVERALL RATING
☆☆☆☆☆

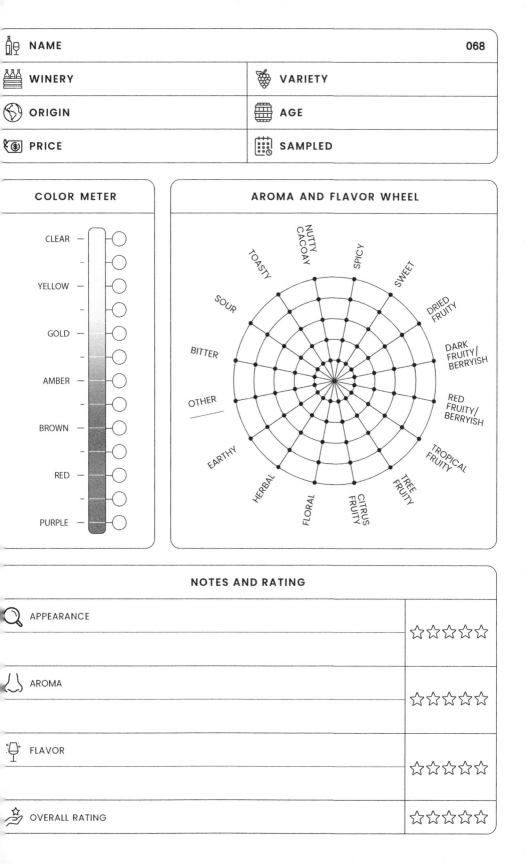

NAME

WINERY	VARIETY
ORIGIN	AGE
PRICE	SAMPLED

COLOR METER

CLEAR
–
YELLOW
–
GOLD
–
AMBER
–
BROWN
–
RED
–
PURPLE

AROMA AND FLAVOR WHEEL

NUTTY CACOAY
TOASTY
SPICY
SOUR
SWEET
BITTER
DRIED FRUITY
OTHER
DARK FRUITY/ BERRYISH
EARTHY
RED FRUITY/ BERRYISH
HERBAL
TROPICAL FRUITY
FLORAL
TREE FRUITY
CITRUS FRUITY

NOTES AND RATING

APPEARANCE
☆☆☆☆☆

AROMA
☆☆☆☆☆

FLAVOR
☆☆☆☆☆

OVERALL RATING
☆☆☆☆☆

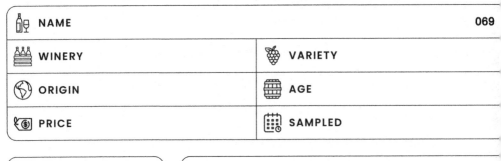

NAME			
WINERY		VARIETY	
ORIGIN		AGE	
PRICE		SAMPLED	

COLOR METER

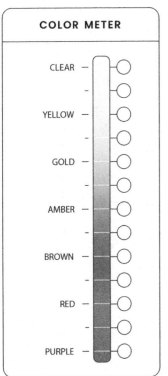

CLEAR
–
YELLOW
–
GOLD
–
AMBER
–
BROWN
–
RED
–
PURPLE

AROMA AND FLAVOR WHEEL

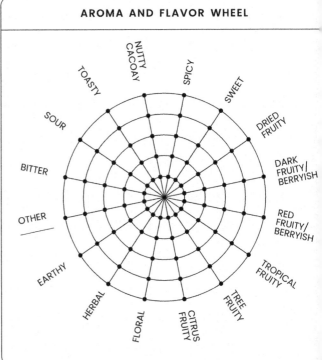

NUTTY CACOAY
SPICY
TOASTY
SWEET
SOUR
DRIED FRUITY
BITTER
DARK FRUITY/BERRYISH
OTHER
RED FRUITY/BERRYISH
EARTHY
TROPICAL FRUITY
HERBAL
TREE FRUITY
FLORAL
CITRUS FRUITY

NOTES AND RATING

APPEARANCE	☆☆☆☆☆
AROMA	☆☆☆☆☆
FLAVOR	☆☆☆☆☆
OVERALL RATING	☆☆☆☆☆

 🍷 NAME	070
🍾 WINERY	🍇 VARIETY
🌍 ORIGIN	🛢 AGE
💲 PRICE	📅 SAMPLED

COLOR METER

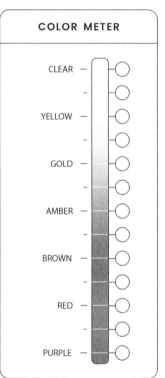

CLEAR

YELLOW

GOLD

AMBER

BROWN

RED

PURPLE

AROMA AND FLAVOR WHEEL

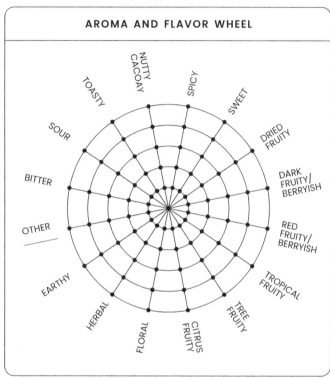

NUTTY CACOAY
TOASTY
SPICY
SOUR
SWEET
BITTER
DRIED FRUITY
OTHER
DARK FRUITY/ BERRYISH
RED FRUITY/ BERRYISH
EARTHY
TROPICAL FRUITY
HERBAL
TREE FRUITY
FLORAL
CITRUS FRUITY

NOTES AND RATING

🔍 APPEARANCE	☆☆☆☆☆
👃 AROMA	☆☆☆☆☆
🍷 FLAVOR	☆☆☆☆☆
🤲 OVERALL RATING	☆☆☆☆☆

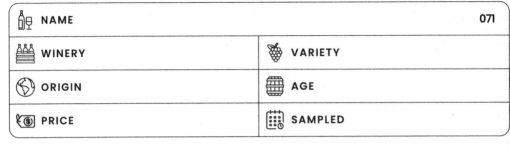

🍾 NAME		071
🍺 WINERY		🍇 VARIETY
🌐 ORIGIN		🛢️ AGE
💰 PRICE		📅 SAMPLED

COLOR METER

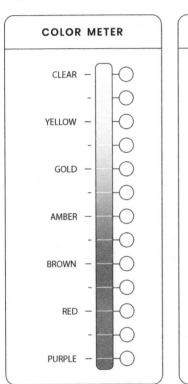

CLEAR —
—
YELLOW —
—
GOLD —
—
AMBER —
—
BROWN —
—
RED —
—
PURPLE —

AROMA AND FLAVOR WHEEL

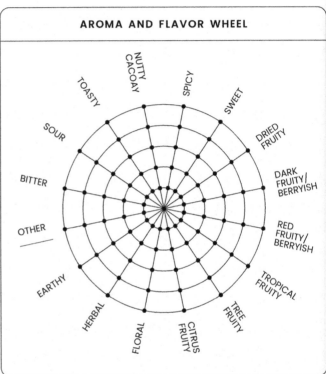

NUTTY CACOAY
SPICY
TOASTY
SWEET
SOUR
DRIED FRUITY
BITTER
DARK FRUITY/BERRYISH
OTHER
RED FRUITY/BERRYISH
TROPICAL FRUITY
EARTHY
TREE FRUITY
HERBAL
CITRUS FRUITY
FLORAL

NOTES AND RATING

🔍 APPEARANCE	☆☆☆☆☆
👃 AROMA	☆☆☆☆☆
🍷 FLAVOR	☆☆☆☆☆
🤲 OVERALL RATING	☆☆☆☆☆

| NAME | 072 |

WINERY	VARIETY
ORIGIN	AGE
PRICE	SAMPLED

COLOR METER

- CLEAR
- YELLOW
- GOLD
- AMBER
- BROWN
- RED
- PURPLE

AROMA AND FLAVOR WHEEL

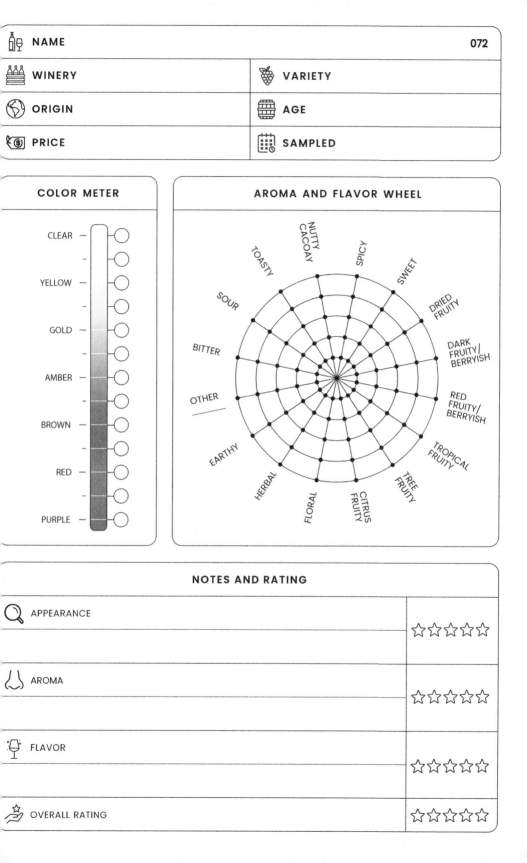

NUTTY CACOAY, TOASTY, SPICY, SOUR, SWEET, BITTER, DRIED FRUITY, OTHER, DARK FRUITY / BERRYISH, EARTHY, RED FRUITY / BERRYISH, HERBAL, TROPICAL FRUITY, FLORAL, CITRUS FRUITY, TREE FRUITY

NOTES AND RATING

APPEARANCE
☆☆☆☆☆

AROMA
☆☆☆☆☆

FLAVOR
☆☆☆☆☆

OVERALL RATING
☆☆☆☆☆

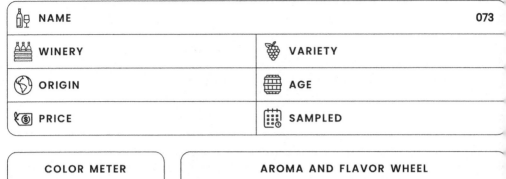

🍾 NAME	073

🍾 WINERY	🍇 VARIETY
🌍 ORIGIN	🛢 AGE
💵 PRICE	📅 SAMPLED

COLOR METER

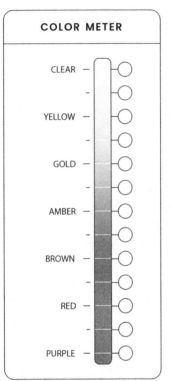

CLEAR —
−
YELLOW —
−
GOLD —
AMBER —
−
BROWN —
−
RED —
−
PURPLE —

AROMA AND FLAVOR WHEEL

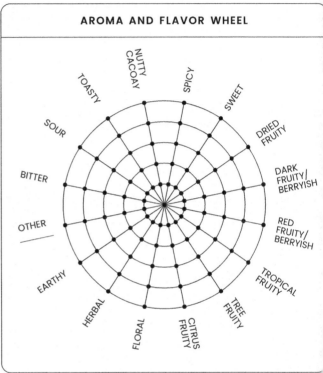

NUTTY CACOAY
TOASTY
SPICY
SOUR
SWEET
BITTER
DRIED FRUITY
OTHER
DARK FRUITY/ BERRYISH
RED FRUITY/ BERRYISH
EARTHY
TROPICAL FRUITY
HERBAL
FLORAL
CITRUS FRUITY
TREE FRUITY

NOTES AND RATING

🔍 APPEARANCE	☆☆☆☆☆

👃 AROMA	☆☆☆☆☆

🥃 FLAVOR	☆☆☆☆☆

🖐 OVERALL RATING	☆☆☆☆☆

🍾 **NAME**	
🍷 **WINERY**	🍇 **VARIETY**
🌐 **ORIGIN**	🛢 **AGE**
💵 **PRICE**	📅 **SAMPLED**

COLOR METER

CLEAR —
—
YELLOW —
—
GOLD —
—
AMBER —
—
BROWN —
—
RED —
—
PURPLE —

AROMA AND FLAVOR WHEEL

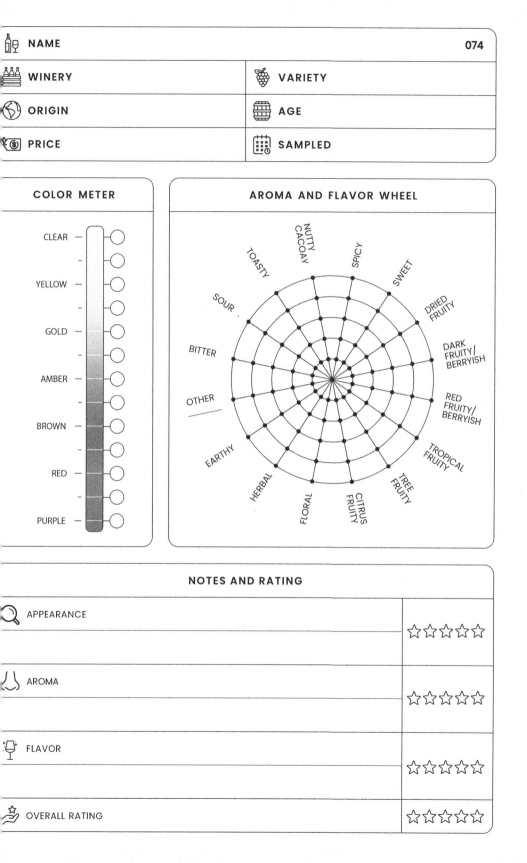

NUTTY
CACOAY
TOASTY
SPICY
SOUR
SWEET
BITTER
DRIED FRUITY
OTHER
DARK FRUITY/ BERRYISH
EARTHY
RED FRUITY/ BERRYISH
HERBAL
TROPICAL FRUITY
FLORAL
TREE FRUITY
CITRUS FRUITY

NOTES AND RATING

🔍 **APPEARANCE**

☆☆☆☆☆

👃 **AROMA**

☆☆☆☆☆

🍷 **FLAVOR**

☆☆☆☆☆

🖐 **OVERALL RATING**

☆☆☆☆☆

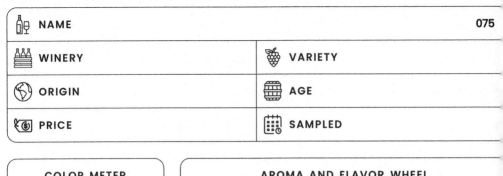

NAME	
WINERY	VARIETY
ORIGIN	AGE
PRICE	SAMPLED

COLOR METER

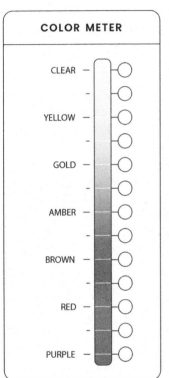

CLEAR —
—
YELLOW —
—
GOLD —
—
AMBER —
—
BROWN —
—
RED —
—
PURPLE —

AROMA AND FLAVOR WHEEL

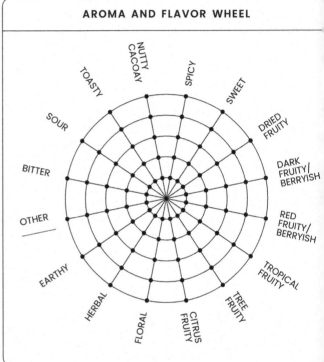

NUTTY CACOAY
SPICY
TOASTY
SWEET
SOUR
DRIED FRUITY
BITTER
DARK FRUITY/BERRYISH
OTHER
RED FRUITY/BERRYISH
TROPICAL FRUITY
EARTHY
TREE FRUITY
HERBAL
FLORAL
CITRUS FRUITY

NOTES AND RATING

APPEARANCE	☆☆☆☆☆
AROMA	☆☆☆☆☆
FLAVOR	☆☆☆☆☆
OVERALL RATING	☆☆☆☆☆

| 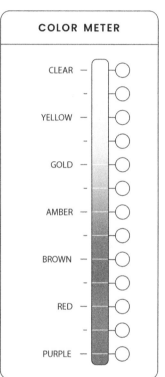 | 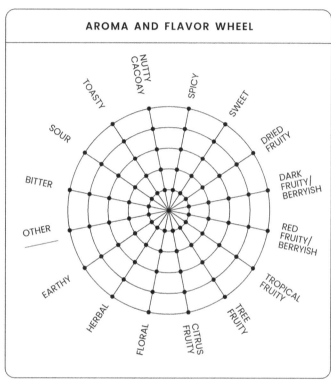 |

NOTES AND RATING

APPEARANCE	☆☆☆☆☆
AROMA	☆☆☆☆☆
FLAVOR	☆☆☆☆☆
OVERALL RATING	☆☆☆☆☆

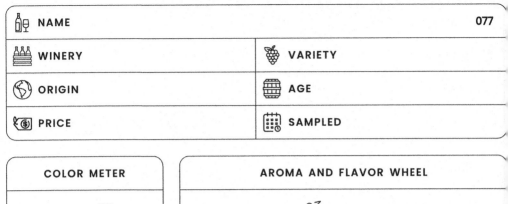

🍾 **NAME**	
🍷 **WINERY**	🍇 **VARIETY**
🌍 **ORIGIN**	🛢 **AGE**
💰 **PRICE**	📅 **SAMPLED**

COLOR METER

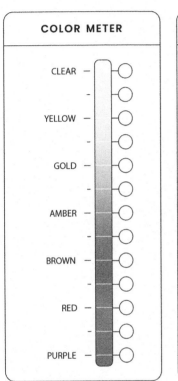

CLEAR
–
YELLOW
–
GOLD
–
AMBER
–
BROWN
–
RED
–
PURPLE

AROMA AND FLAVOR WHEEL

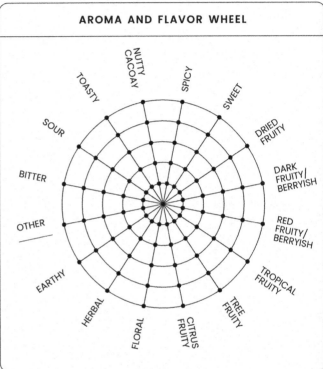

NUTTY CACOAY · SPICY · SWEET · DRIED FRUITY · DARK FRUITY/BERRYISH · RED FRUITY/BERRYISH · TROPICAL FRUITY · TREE FRUITY · CITRUS FRUITY · FLORAL · HERBAL · EARTHY · OTHER · BITTER · SOUR · TOASTY

NOTES AND RATING

🔍 APPEARANCE	☆☆☆☆☆
👃 AROMA	☆☆☆☆☆
🍷 FLAVOR	☆☆☆☆☆
🙌 OVERALL RATING	☆☆☆☆☆

🍾 **NAME**	**078**

🍾 **WINERY**	🍇 **VARIETY**	
🌐 **ORIGIN**	🛢️ **AGE**	
💵 **PRICE**	📅 **SAMPLED**	

COLOR METER

CLEAR —
–
YELLOW —
–
GOLD —
–
AMBER —
–
BROWN —
–
RED —
–
PURPLE —

AROMA AND FLAVOR WHEEL

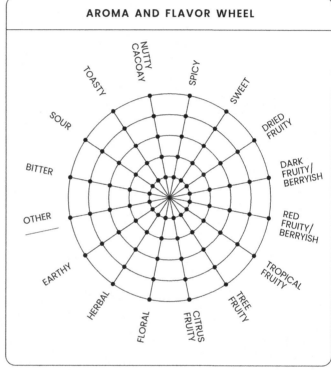

NUTTY CACOAY
SPICY
TOASTY
SWEET
SOUR
DRIED FRUITY
BITTER
DARK FRUITY / BERRYISH
OTHER
RED FRUITY / BERRYISH
EARTHY
TROPICAL FRUITY
HERBAL
TREE FRUITY
FLORAL
CITRUS FRUITY

NOTES AND RATING

🔍 **APPEARANCE**
☆☆☆☆☆

👃 **AROMA**
☆☆☆☆☆

🍷 **FLAVOR**
☆☆☆☆☆

🤲 **OVERALL RATING**
☆☆☆☆☆

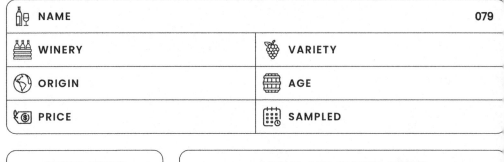

🍷 NAME		079
🍾 WINERY	🍇 VARIETY	
🌍 ORIGIN	🛢 AGE	
💵 PRICE	📅 SAMPLED	

COLOR METER

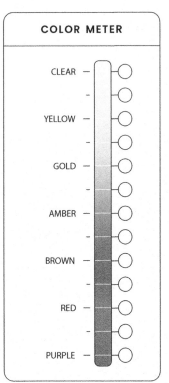

CLEAR —
—
YELLOW —
—
GOLD —
—
AMBER —
—
BROWN —
—
RED —
—
PURPLE —

AROMA AND FLAVOR WHEEL

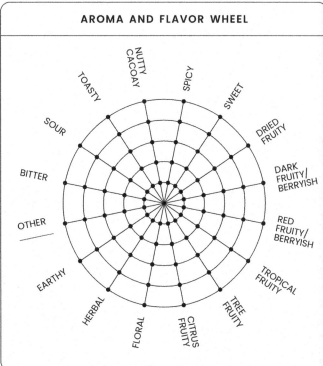

NUTTY CACOAY
TOASTY
SPICY
SWEET
SOUR
DRIED FRUITY
BITTER
DARK FRUITY/ BERRYISH
OTHER
RED FRUITY/ BERRYISH
EARTHY
TROPICAL FRUITY
HERBAL
TREE FRUITY
FLORAL
CITRUS FRUITY

NOTES AND RATING

🔍 APPEARANCE	☆☆☆☆☆
👃 AROMA	☆☆☆☆☆
🍷 FLAVOR	☆☆☆☆☆
🖐 OVERALL RATING	☆☆☆☆☆

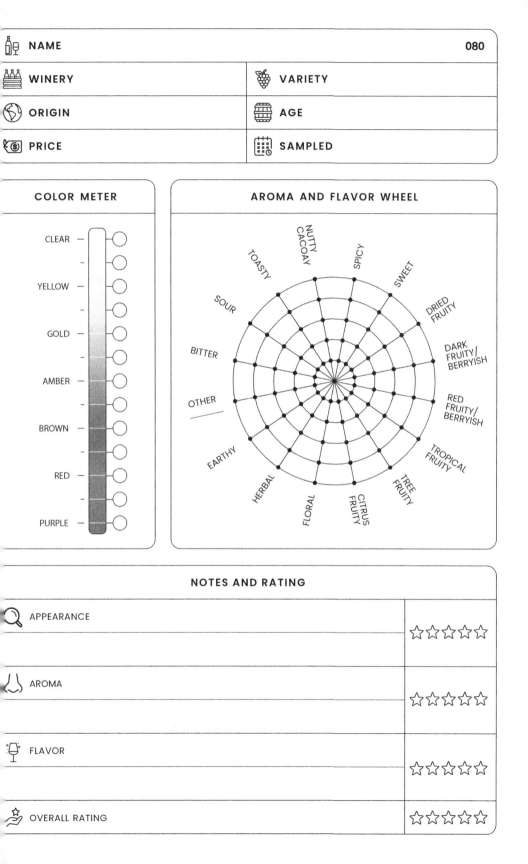

NAME

080

WINERY

VARIETY

ORIGIN

AGE

PRICE

SAMPLED

COLOR METER

CLEAR –
–
YELLOW –
–
GOLD –
–
AMBER –
–
BROWN –
–
RED –
–
PURPLE –

AROMA AND FLAVOR WHEEL

NUTTY
CACOAY
TOASTY
SPICY
SOUR
SWEET
BITTER
DRIED FRUITY
OTHER
DARK FRUITY/BERRYISH
RED FRUITY/BERRYISH
EARTHY
TROPICAL FRUITY
HERBAL
TREE FRUITY
FLORAL
CITRUS FRUITY

NOTES AND RATING

APPEARANCE
☆☆☆☆☆

AROMA
☆☆☆☆☆

FLAVOR
☆☆☆☆☆

OVERALL RATING
☆☆☆☆☆

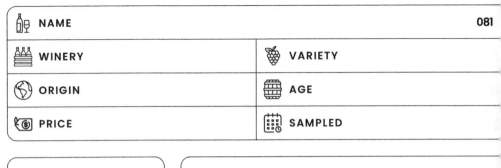

NAME			
WINERY		**VARIETY**	
ORIGIN		**AGE**	
PRICE		**SAMPLED**	

COLOR METER

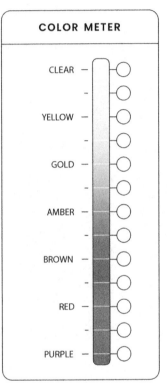

CLEAR —
—
YELLOW —
—
GOLD —
—
AMBER —
—
BROWN —
—
RED —
—
PURPLE —

AROMA AND FLAVOR WHEEL

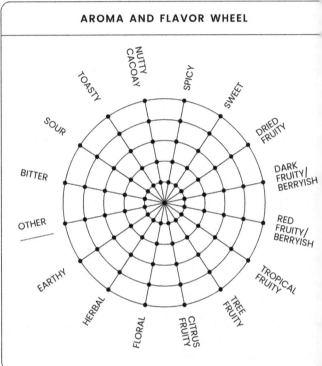

NUTTY CACOAY · SPICY · SWEET · DRIED FRUITY · DARK FRUITY/BERRYISH · RED FRUITY/BERRYISH · TROPICAL FRUITY · TREE FRUITY · CITRUS FRUITY · FLORAL · HERBAL · EARTHY · OTHER · BITTER · SOUR · TOASTY

NOTES AND RATING

APPEARANCE ☆☆☆☆☆

AROMA ☆☆☆☆☆

FLAVOR ☆☆☆☆☆

OVERALL RATING ☆☆☆☆☆

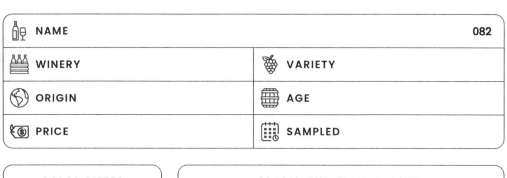

 🍷 **NAME**	**082**
🍾 **WINERY**	🍇 **VARIETY**
🌍 **ORIGIN**	🛢 **AGE**
💲 **PRICE**	📅 **SAMPLED**

COLOR METER

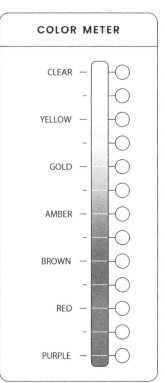

CLEAR —
—
YELLOW —
—
GOLD —
—
AMBER —
—
BROWN —
—
RED —
—
PURPLE —

AROMA AND FLAVOR WHEEL

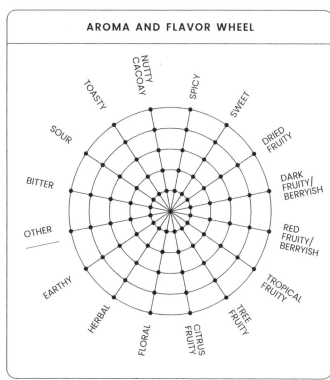

NUTTY CACOAY
TOASTY
SPICY
SOUR
SWEET
BITTER
DRIED FRUITY
OTHER
DARK FRUITY/ BERRYISH
EARTHY
RED FRUITY/ BERRYISH
HERBAL
TROPICAL FRUITY
FLORAL
TREE FRUITY
CITRUS FRUITY

NOTES AND RATING

🔍 **APPEARANCE**
☆☆☆☆☆

👃 **AROMA**
☆☆☆☆☆

🍷 **FLAVOR**
☆☆☆☆☆

🤲 **OVERALL RATING**
☆☆☆☆☆

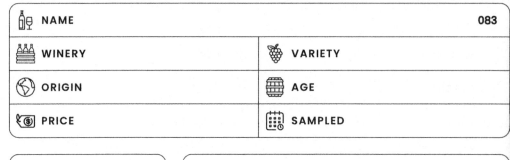	
NAME	
WINERY	VARIETY
ORIGIN	AGE
PRICE	SAMPLED

COLOR METER

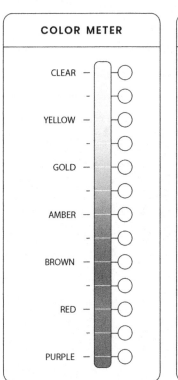

- CLEAR
- –
- YELLOW
- –
- GOLD
- –
- AMBER
- –
- BROWN
- –
- RED
- –
- PURPLE

AROMA AND FLAVOR WHEEL

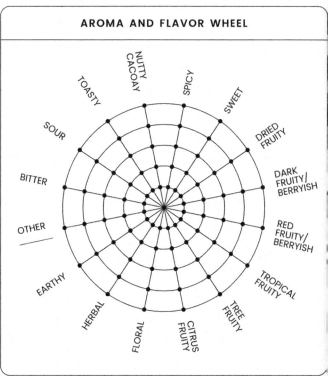

NUTTY CACOAY · SPICY · SWEET · DRIED FRUITY · DARK FRUITY/BERRYISH · RED FRUITY/BERRYISH · TROPICAL FRUITY · TREE FRUITY · CITRUS FRUITY · FLORAL · HERBAL · EARTHY · OTHER · BITTER · SOUR · TOASTY

NOTES AND RATING

APPEARANCE	☆☆☆☆☆
AROMA	☆☆☆☆☆
FLAVOR	☆☆☆☆☆
OVERALL RATING	☆☆☆☆☆

🍾 **NAME**		**084**

🍾 **WINERY**	🍇 **VARIETY**	
🌍 **ORIGIN**	🛢 **AGE**	
💰 **PRICE**	📅 **SAMPLED**	

COLOR METER

- CLEAR
- —
- YELLOW
- —
- GOLD
- —
- AMBER
- —
- BROWN
- —
- RED
- —
- PURPLE

AROMA AND FLAVOR WHEEL

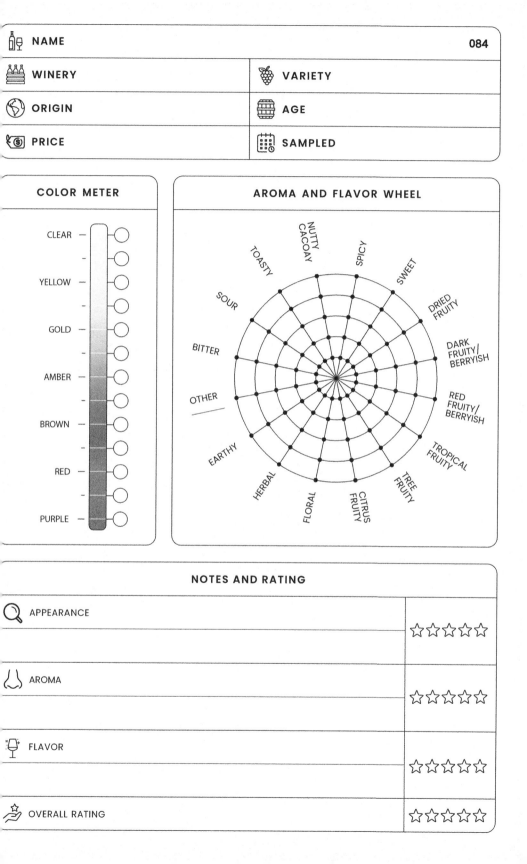

NUTTY CACOAY · TOASTY · SPICY · SOUR · SWEET · BITTER · DRIED FRUITY · OTHER · DARK FRUITY/BERRYISH · RED FRUITY/BERRYISH · EARTHY · TROPICAL FRUITY · HERBAL · TREE FRUITY · FLORAL · CITRUS FRUITY

NOTES AND RATING

🔍 **APPEARANCE**

☆☆☆☆☆

👃 **AROMA**

☆☆☆☆☆

🍷 **FLAVOR**

☆☆☆☆☆

⭐ **OVERALL RATING**

☆☆☆☆☆

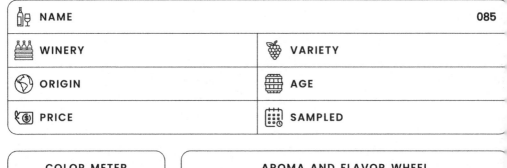

NAME		085
WINERY	VARIETY	
ORIGIN	AGE	
PRICE	SAMPLED	

COLOR METER

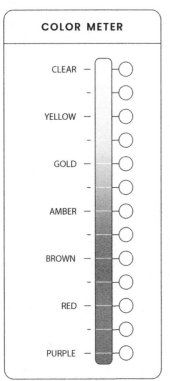

CLEAR —
-
YELLOW —
-
GOLD —
-
AMBER —
-
BROWN —
-
RED —
-
PURPLE —

AROMA AND FLAVOR WHEEL

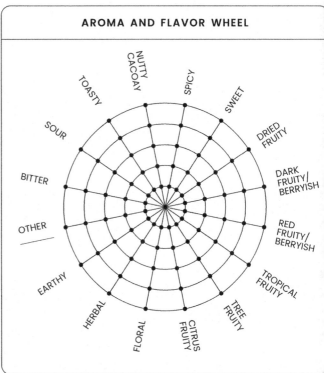

NUTTY CACOAY
TOASTY
SPICY
SOUR
SWEET
BITTER
DRIED FRUITY
OTHER
DARK FRUITY/ BERRYISH
EARTHY
RED FRUITY/ BERRYISH
HERBAL
TROPICAL FRUITY
FLORAL
CITRUS FRUITY
TREE FRUITY

NOTES AND RATING

APPEARANCE
☆☆☆☆☆

AROMA
☆☆☆☆☆

FLAVOR
☆☆☆☆☆

OVERALL RATING
☆☆☆☆☆

NAME

WINERY	VARIETY
ORIGIN	AGE
PRICE	SAMPLED

COLOR METER

- CLEAR
- –
- YELLOW
- –
- GOLD
- –
- AMBER
- –
- BROWN
- –
- RED
- –
- PURPLE

AROMA AND FLAVOR WHEEL

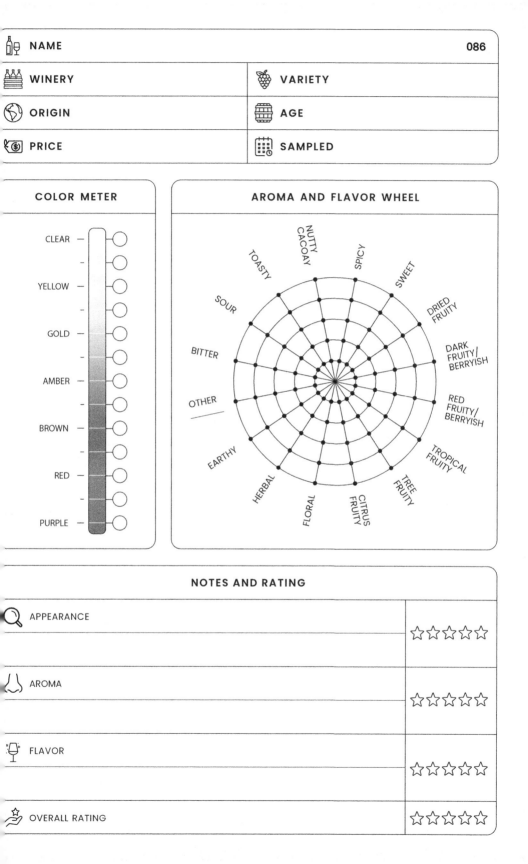

NUTTY CACOAY · SPICY · SWEET · DRIED FRUITY · DARK FRUITY/BERRYISH · RED FRUITY/BERRYISH · TROPICAL FRUITY · TREE FRUITY · CITRUS FRUITY · FLORAL · HERBAL · EARTHY · OTHER · BITTER · SOUR · TOASTY

NOTES AND RATING

APPEARANCE ☆☆☆☆☆

AROMA ☆☆☆☆☆

FLAVOR ☆☆☆☆☆

OVERALL RATING ☆☆☆☆☆

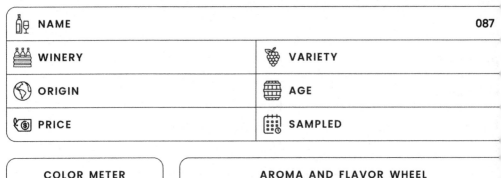

🍷 NAME	
🍾 WINERY	🍇 VARIETY
🌐 ORIGIN	🛢️ AGE
💲 PRICE	📅 SAMPLED

COLOR METER

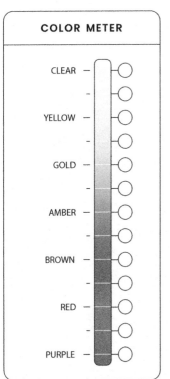

- CLEAR
- –
- YELLOW
- –
- GOLD
- –
- AMBER
- –
- BROWN
- –
- RED
- –
- PURPLE

AROMA AND FLAVOR WHEEL

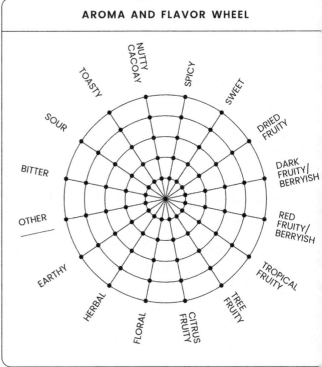

NUTTY CACOAY · SPICY · SWEET · DRIED FRUITY · DARK FRUITY/BERRYISH · RED FRUITY/BERRYISH · TROPICAL FRUITY · TREE FRUITY · CITRUS FRUITY · FLORAL · HERBAL · EARTHY · OTHER · BITTER · SOUR · TOASTY

NOTES AND RATING

🔍 APPEARANCE	☆☆☆☆☆
👃 AROMA	☆☆☆☆☆
🍷 FLAVOR	☆☆☆☆☆
🤲 OVERALL RATING	☆☆☆☆☆

 NAME		088
WINERY	VARIETY	
ORIGIN	AGE	
PRICE	SAMPLED	

COLOR METER

- CLEAR
- —
- YELLOW
- —
- GOLD
- —
- AMBER
- —
- BROWN
- —
- RED
- —
- PURPLE

AROMA AND FLAVOR WHEEL

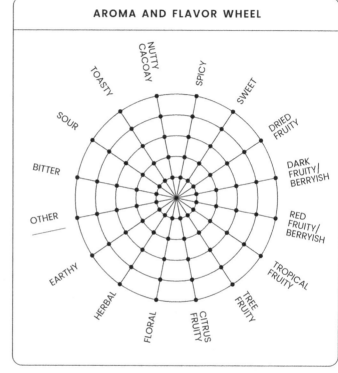

NUTTY CACOAY · SPICY · SWEET · DRIED FRUITY · DARK FRUITY/BERRYISH · RED FRUITY/BERRYISH · TROPICAL FRUITY · TREE FRUITY · CITRUS FRUITY · FLORAL · HERBAL · EARTHY · OTHER · BITTER · SOUR · TOASTY

NOTES AND RATING

APPEARANCE	☆☆☆☆☆
AROMA	☆☆☆☆☆
FLAVOR	☆☆☆☆☆
OVERALL RATING	☆☆☆☆☆

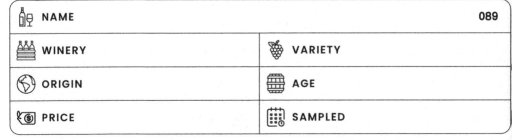

  NAME		089
WINERY	VARIETY	
ORIGIN	AGE	
PRICE	SAMPLED	

COLOR METER

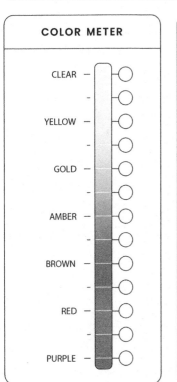

CLEAR

YELLOW

GOLD

AMBER

BROWN

RED

PURPLE

AROMA AND FLAVOR WHEEL

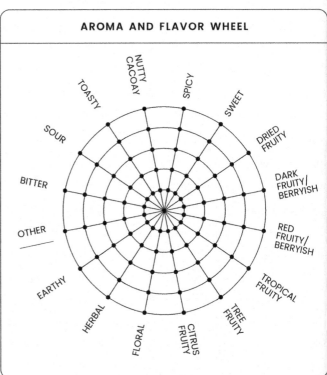

NUTTY CACOAY · SPICY · SWEET · DRIED FRUITY · DARK FRUITY/BERRYISH · RED FRUITY/BERRYISH · TROPICAL FRUITY · TREE FRUITY · CITRUS FRUITY · FLORAL · HERBAL · EARTHY · OTHER · BITTER · SOUR · TOASTY

NOTES AND RATING

APPEARANCE	☆☆☆☆☆
AROMA	☆☆☆☆☆
FLAVOR	☆☆☆☆☆
OVERALL RATING	☆☆☆☆☆

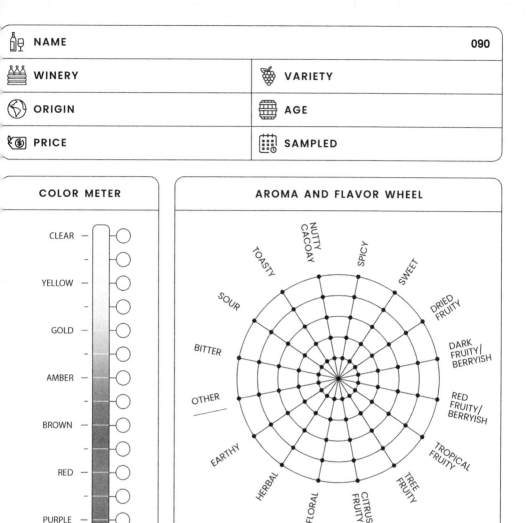 NAME	090

WINERY	VARIETY
ORIGIN	AGE
PRICE	SAMPLED

COLOR METER

- CLEAR
- —
- YELLOW
- —
- GOLD
- —
- AMBER
- —
- BROWN
- —
- RED
- —
- PURPLE

AROMA AND FLAVOR WHEEL

NUTTY CACOAY
TOASTY
SPICY
SOUR
SWEET
BITTER
DRIED FRUITY
OTHER
DARK FRUITY / BERRYISH
EARTHY
RED FRUITY / BERRYISH
HERBAL
TROPICAL FRUITY
FLORAL
TREE FRUITY
CITRUS FRUITY

NOTES AND RATING

APPEARANCE	☆☆☆☆☆
AROMA	☆☆☆☆☆
FLAVOR	☆☆☆☆☆
OVERALL RATING	☆☆☆☆☆

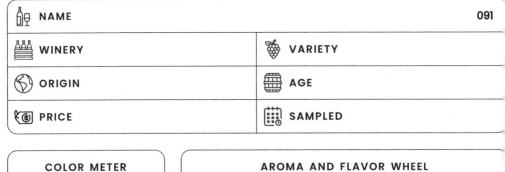

🍾 **NAME**		091
🍾 **WINERY**	🍇 **VARIETY**	
🌐 **ORIGIN**	🛢 **AGE**	
💵 **PRICE**	📅 **SAMPLED**	

COLOR METER

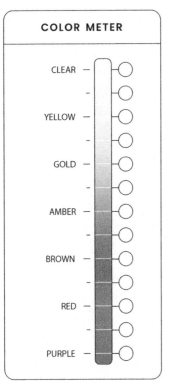

AROMA AND FLAVOR WHEEL

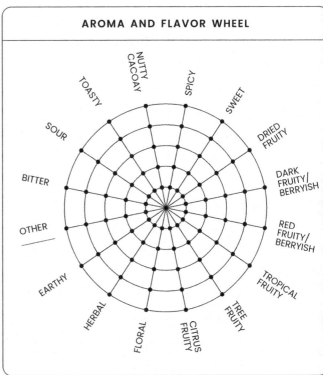

NOTES AND RATING

🔍 **APPEARANCE**

☆☆☆☆☆

👃 **AROMA**

☆☆☆☆☆

🍷 **FLAVOR**

☆☆☆☆☆

🤲 **OVERALL RATING**

☆☆☆☆☆

NAME

WINERY	VARIETY
ORIGIN	AGE
PRICE	SAMPLED

COLOR METER

- CLEAR
- –
- YELLOW
- –
- GOLD
- –
- AMBER
- –
- BROWN
- –
- RED
- –
- PURPLE

AROMA AND FLAVOR WHEEL

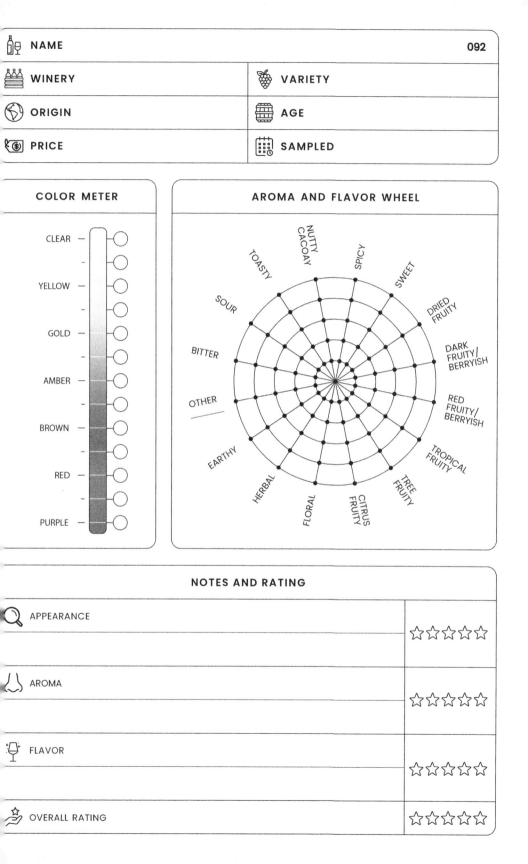

NUTTY CACOAY · SPICY · SWEET · DRIED FRUITY · DARK FRUITY/BERRYISH · RED FRUITY/BERRYISH · TROPICAL FRUITY · TREE FRUITY · CITRUS FRUITY · FLORAL · HERBAL · EARTHY · OTHER · BITTER · SOUR · TOASTY

NOTES AND RATING

APPEARANCE
☆☆☆☆☆

AROMA
☆☆☆☆☆

FLAVOR
☆☆☆☆☆

OVERALL RATING
☆☆☆☆☆

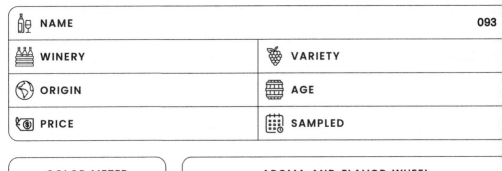

	093
🍷 NAME	
🍾 WINERY	🍇 VARIETY
🌐 ORIGIN	🛢️ AGE
💵 PRICE	📅 SAMPLED

COLOR METER

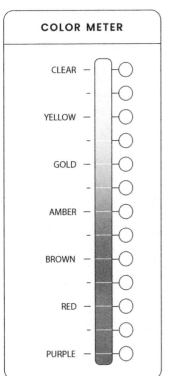

CLEAR
YELLOW
GOLD
AMBER
BROWN
RED
PURPLE

AROMA AND FLAVOR WHEEL

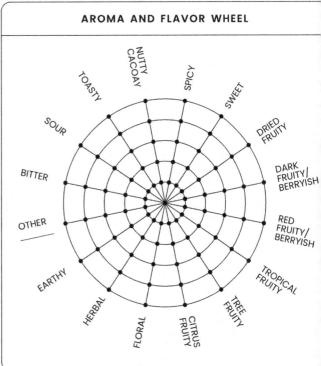

NUTTY CACOAY
TOASTY
SPICY
SOUR
SWEET
DRIED FRUITY
BITTER
DARK FRUITY/ BERRYISH
OTHER
RED FRUITY/ BERRYISH
EARTHY
TROPICAL FRUITY
HERBAL
TREE FRUITY
FLORAL
CITRUS FRUITY

NOTES AND RATING

🔍 APPEARANCE	☆☆☆☆☆
👃 AROMA	☆☆☆☆☆
🍷 FLAVOR	☆☆☆☆☆
🏆 OVERALL RATING	☆☆☆☆☆

 🍾 **NAME**	094
🍷 **WINERY**	🍇 **VARIETY**
🌍 **ORIGIN**	🛢 **AGE**
💲 **PRICE**	📅 **SAMPLED**

COLOR METER

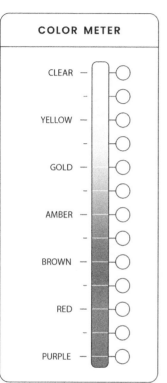

CLEAR —
—
YELLOW —
—
GOLD —
—
AMBER —
—
BROWN —
—
RED —
—
PURPLE —

AROMA AND FLAVOR WHEEL

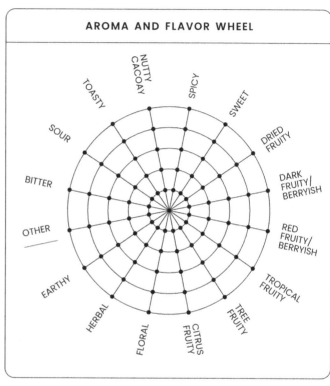

NUTTY CACOAY • SPICY • TOASTY • SWEET • SOUR • DRIED FRUITY • BITTER • DARK FRUITY/BERRYISH • OTHER • RED FRUITY/BERRYISH • EARTHY • TROPICAL FRUITY • HERBAL • TREE FRUITY • FLORAL • CITRUS FRUITY

NOTES AND RATING

🔍 **APPEARANCE**

☆☆☆☆☆

👃 **AROMA**

☆☆☆☆☆

🍷 **FLAVOR**

☆☆☆☆☆

🤲 **OVERALL RATING**

☆☆☆☆☆

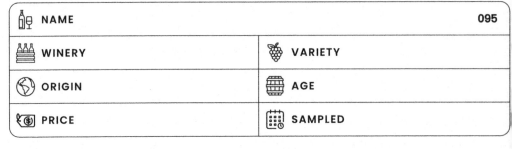

🍾 **NAME**		095
🍾 **WINERY**	🍇 **VARIETY**	
🌍 **ORIGIN**	🛢 **AGE**	
💲 **PRICE**	📅 **SAMPLED**	

COLOR METER

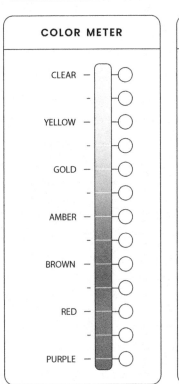

CLEAR

YELLOW

GOLD

AMBER

BROWN

RED

PURPLE

AROMA AND FLAVOR WHEEL

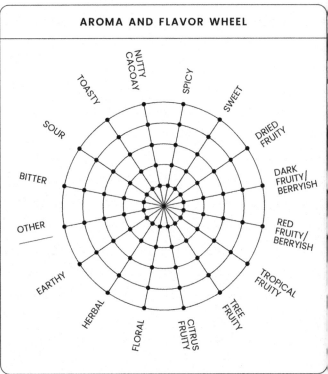

NUTTY CACOAY · SPICY · SWEET · DRIED FRUITY · DARK FRUITY/BERRYISH · RED FRUITY/BERRYISH · TROPICAL FRUITY · TREE FRUITY · CITRUS FRUITY · FLORAL · HERBAL · EARTHY · OTHER · BITTER · SOUR · TOASTY

NOTES AND RATING

🔍 APPEARANCE	☆☆☆☆☆
👃 AROMA	☆☆☆☆☆
🍷 FLAVOR	☆☆☆☆☆
🙌 OVERALL RATING	☆☆☆☆☆

🍾 **NAME**	**096**

🍾 **WINERY**		🍇 **VARIETY**	
🌐 **ORIGIN**		🛢 **AGE**	
💰 **PRICE**		📅 **SAMPLED**	

COLOR METER

CLEAR —
—
YELLOW —
—
GOLD —
—
AMBER —
—
BROWN —
—
RED —
—
PURPLE —

AROMA AND FLAVOR WHEEL

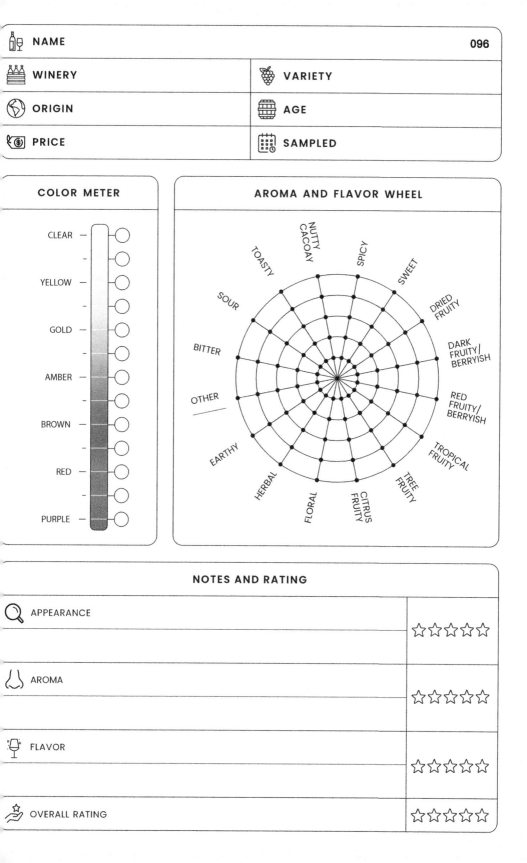

NUTTY CACOAY · SPICY · SWEET · DRIED FRUITY · DARK FRUITY/BERRYISH · RED FRUITY/BERRYISH · TROPICAL FRUITY · TREE FRUITY · CITRUS FRUITY · FLORAL · HERBAL · EARTHY · OTHER · BITTER · SOUR · TOASTY

NOTES AND RATING

🔍 **APPEARANCE**

☆☆☆☆☆

👃 **AROMA**

☆☆☆☆☆

🍷 **FLAVOR**

☆☆☆☆☆

🖐 **OVERALL RATING**

☆☆☆☆☆

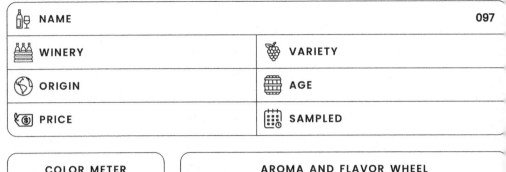

🍾 NAME		097
🍾 WINERY		🍇 VARIETY
🌍 ORIGIN		🛢 AGE
💵 PRICE		📅 SAMPLED

COLOR METER

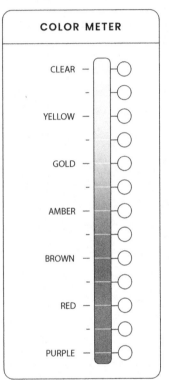

CLEAR —
—
YELLOW —
—
GOLD —
—
AMBER —
—
BROWN —
—
RED —
—
PURPLE —

AROMA AND FLAVOR WHEEL

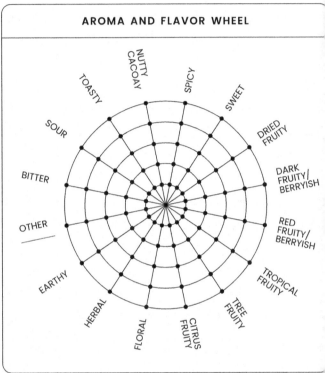

NUTTY CACOAY
SPICY
SWEET
TOASTY
DRIED FRUITY
SOUR
DARK FRUITY/BERRYISH
BITTER
OTHER
RED FRUITY/BERRYISH
EARTHY
TROPICAL FRUITY
HERBAL
FLORAL
CITRUS FRUITY
TREE FRUITY

NOTES AND RATING

🔍 APPEARANCE	☆☆☆☆☆
👃 AROMA	☆☆☆☆☆
🥃 FLAVOR	☆☆☆☆☆
🙌 OVERALL RATING	☆☆☆☆☆

🍾 NAME	
🍷 WINERY	🍇 VARIETY
🌍 ORIGIN	🛢 AGE
💰 PRICE	📅 SAMPLED

COLOR METER

- CLEAR
- –
- YELLOW
- –
- GOLD
- –
- AMBER
- –
- BROWN
- –
- RED
- –
- PURPLE

AROMA AND FLAVOR WHEEL

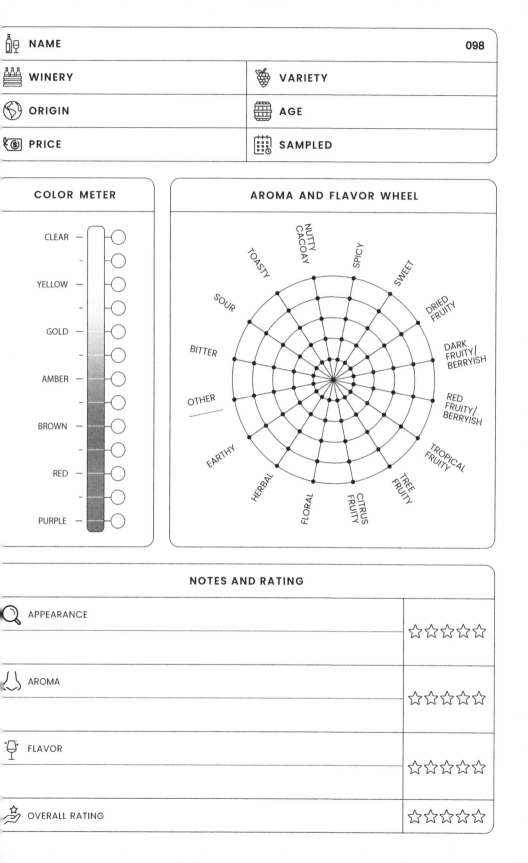

NUTTY CACOAY · SPICY · TOASTY · SWEET · SOUR · DRIED FRUITY · BITTER · DARK FRUITY/BERRYISH · OTHER · RED FRUITY/BERRYISH · EARTHY · TROPICAL FRUITY · HERBAL · TREE FRUITY · FLORAL · CITRUS FRUITY

NOTES AND RATING

🔍 APPEARANCE
☆☆☆☆☆

👃 AROMA
☆☆☆☆☆

🥃 FLAVOR
☆☆☆☆☆

🖐 OVERALL RATING
☆☆☆☆☆

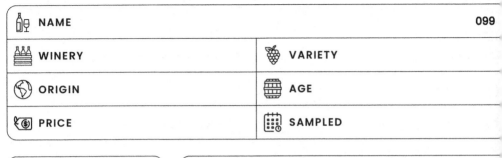

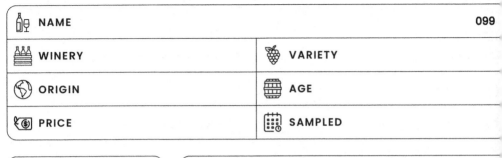 NAME	
WINERY	VARIETY
ORIGIN	AGE
PRICE	SAMPLED

COLOR METER

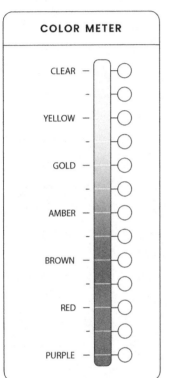

CLEAR —

YELLOW —

GOLD —

AMBER —

BROWN —

RED —

PURPLE —

AROMA AND FLAVOR WHEEL

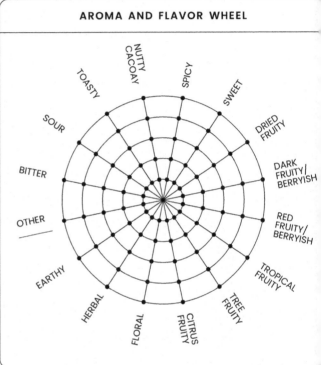

NUTTY CACOAY
SPICY
TOASTY
SWEET
SOUR
DRIED FRUITY
BITTER
DARK FRUITY/ BERRYISH
OTHER
RED FRUITY/ BERRYISH
EARTHY
TROPICAL FRUITY
HERBAL
TREE FRUITY
FLORAL
CITRUS FRUITY

NOTES AND RATING

APPEARANCE	☆☆☆☆☆
AROMA	☆☆☆☆☆
FLAVOR	☆☆☆☆☆
OVERALL RATING	☆☆☆☆☆

🍾 NAME		100
🍶 WINERY	🍇 VARIETY	
🌍 ORIGIN	🛢 AGE	
💲 PRICE	📅 SAMPLED	

COLOR METER

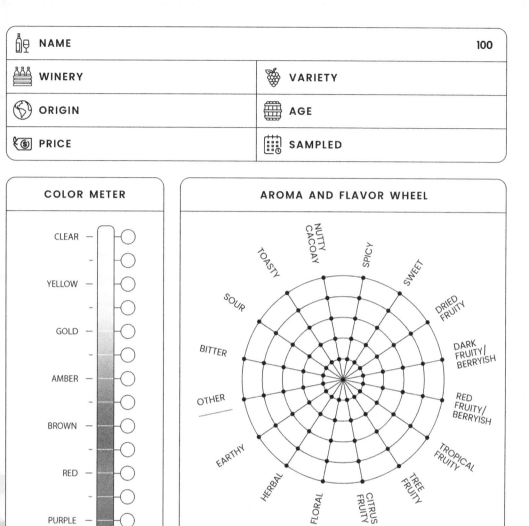

CLEAR

YELLOW

GOLD

AMBER

BROWN

RED

PURPLE

AROMA AND FLAVOR WHEEL

TOASTY — NUTTY CACAOY — SPICY — SWEET — DRIED FRUITY — DARK FRUITY/BERRYISH — RED FRUITY/BERRYISH — TROPICAL FRUITY — TREE FRUITY — CITRUS FRUITY — FLORAL — HERBAL — EARTHY — OTHER — BITTER — SOUR

NOTES AND RATING

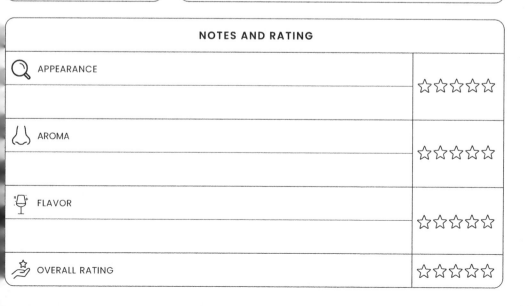

🔍 APPEARANCE

☆☆☆☆☆

👃 AROMA

☆☆☆☆☆

🍷 FLAVOR

☆☆☆☆☆

🤲 OVERALL RATING

☆☆☆☆☆

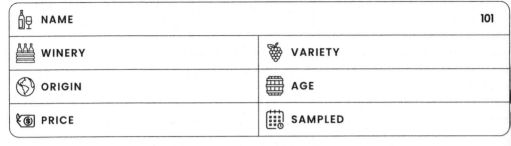

 🍾 NAME	101
🍻 WINERY	🍇 VARIETY
🌍 ORIGIN	🛢 AGE
💵 PRICE	📅 SAMPLED

COLOR METER

CLEAR —
–
YELLOW —
–
GOLD —
–
AMBER —
–
BROWN —
–
RED —
–
PURPLE —

AROMA AND FLAVOR WHEEL

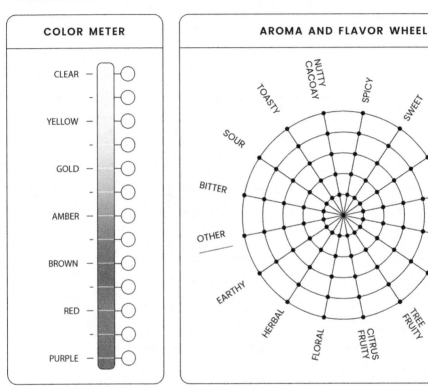

NUTTY CACOAY
TOASTY
SPICY
SOUR
SWEET
BITTER
DRIED FRUITY
OTHER
DARK FRUITY/ BERRYISH
EARTHY
RED FRUITY/ BERRYISH
HERBAL
TROPICAL FRUITY
FLORAL
TREE FRUITY
CITRUS FRUITY

NOTES AND RATING

🔍 APPEARANCE	☆☆☆☆☆
👃 AROMA	☆☆☆☆☆
🍷 FLAVOR	☆☆☆☆☆
🖐 OVERALL RATING	☆☆☆☆☆

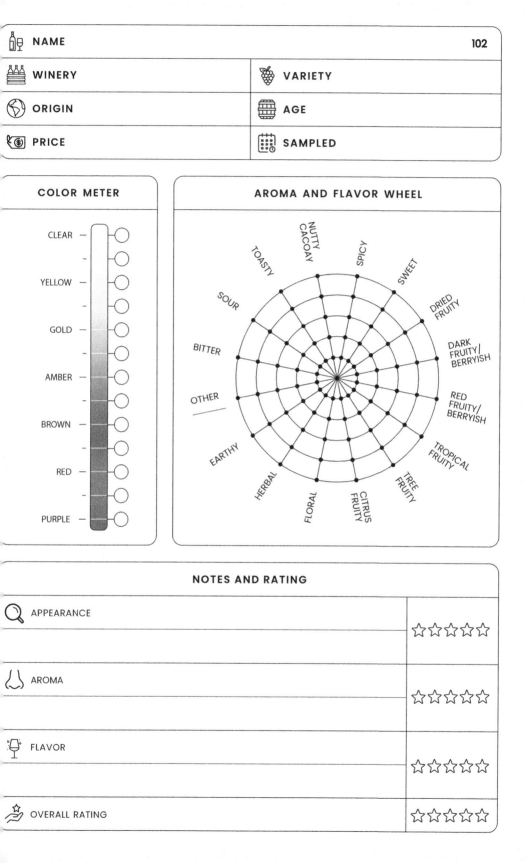 NAME		102

WINERY	VARIETY
ORIGIN	AGE
PRICE	SAMPLED

COLOR METER

- CLEAR
- —
- YELLOW
- —
- GOLD
- —
- AMBER
- —
- BROWN
- —
- RED
- —
- PURPLE

AROMA AND FLAVOR WHEEL

NUTTY CACOAY
TOASTY
SPICY
SWEET
SOUR
DRIED FRUITY
BITTER
DARK FRUITY/ BERRYISH
OTHER
RED FRUITY/ BERRYISH
EARTHY
TROPICAL FRUITY
HERBAL
TREE FRUITY
FLORAL
CITRUS FRUITY

NOTES AND RATING

APPEARANCE	☆☆☆☆☆
AROMA	☆☆☆☆☆
FLAVOR	☆☆☆☆☆
OVERALL RATING	☆☆☆☆☆

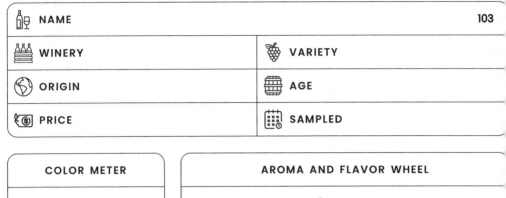

NAME	
WINERY	VARIETY
ORIGIN	AGE
PRICE	SAMPLED

COLOR METER

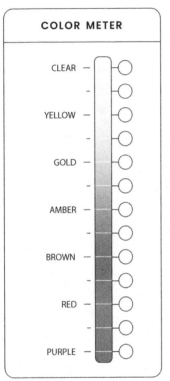

CLEAR —
–
YELLOW —
–
GOLD —
–
AMBER —
–
BROWN —
–
RED —
–
PURPLE —

AROMA AND FLAVOR WHEEL

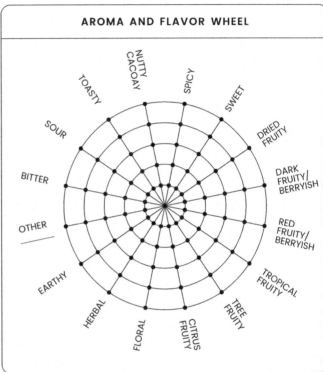

NUTTY CACOAY
TOASTY
SPICY
SWEET
SOUR
DRIED FRUITY
BITTER
DARK FRUITY/ BERRYISH
OTHER
RED FRUITY/ BERRYISH
EARTHY
TROPICAL FRUITY
HERBAL
TREE FRUITY
FLORAL
CITRUS FRUITY

NOTES AND RATING

APPEARANCE	☆☆☆☆☆
AROMA	☆☆☆☆☆
FLAVOR	☆☆☆☆☆
OVERALL RATING	☆☆☆☆☆

🍾 NAME	
🍷 WINERY	🍇 VARIETY
🌍 ORIGIN	🛢 AGE
💲 PRICE	📅 SAMPLED

COLOR METER

- CLEAR
- –
- YELLOW
- –
- GOLD
- –
- AMBER
- –
- BROWN
- –
- RED
- –
- PURPLE

AROMA AND FLAVOR WHEEL

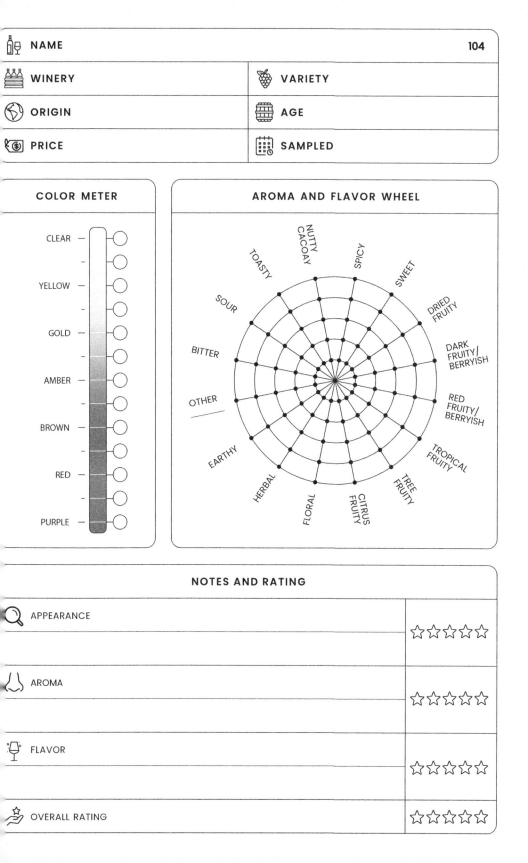

NUTTY CACOAY · SPICY · SWEET · DRIED FRUITY · DARK FRUITY/BERRYISH · RED FRUITY/BERRYISH · TROPICAL FRUITY · TREE FRUITY · CITRUS FRUITY · FLORAL · HERBAL · EARTHY · OTHER · BITTER · SOUR · TOASTY

NOTES AND RATING

🔍 APPEARANCE
☆☆☆☆☆

👃 AROMA
☆☆☆☆☆

🍷 FLAVOR
☆☆☆☆☆

🙌 OVERALL RATING
☆☆☆☆☆

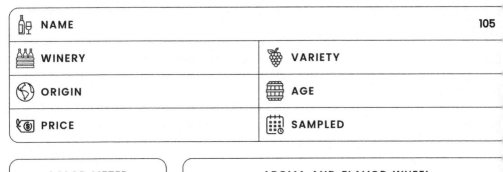 NAME	
WINERY	VARIETY
ORIGIN	AGE
PRICE	SAMPLED

COLOR METER

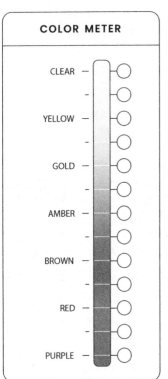

CLEAR —
—
YELLOW —
—
GOLD —
—
AMBER —
—
BROWN —
—
RED —
—
PURPLE —

AROMA AND FLAVOR WHEEL

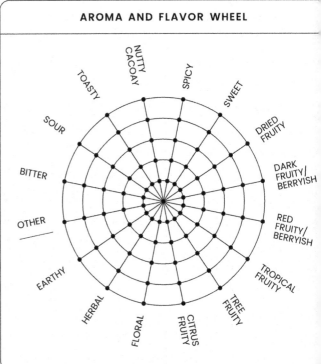

NUTTY
CACOAY
SPICY
TOASTY
SWEET
SOUR
DRIED FRUITY
BITTER
DARK FRUITY/ BERRYISH
OTHER
RED FRUITY/ BERRYISH
EARTHY
TROPICAL FRUITY
HERBAL
TREE FRUITY
FLORAL
CITRUS FRUITY

NOTES AND RATING

APPEARANCE		☆☆☆☆☆
AROMA		☆☆☆☆☆
FLAVOR		☆☆☆☆☆
OVERALL RATING		☆☆☆☆☆

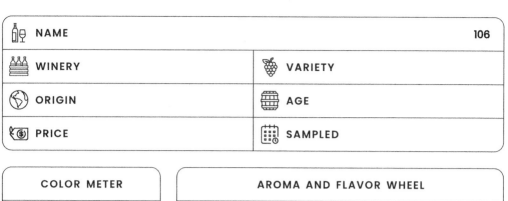	
NAME	
WINERY	**VARIETY**
ORIGIN	**AGE**
PRICE	**SAMPLED**

COLOR METER

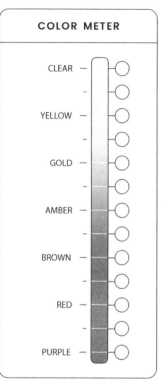

CLEAR

YELLOW

GOLD

AMBER

BROWN

RED

PURPLE

AROMA AND FLAVOR WHEEL

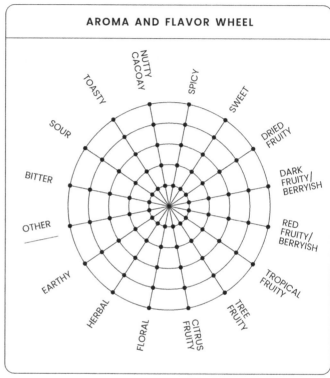

NOTES AND RATING

APPEARANCE	☆☆☆☆☆
AROMA	☆☆☆☆☆
FLAVOR	☆☆☆☆☆
OVERALL RATING	☆☆☆☆☆

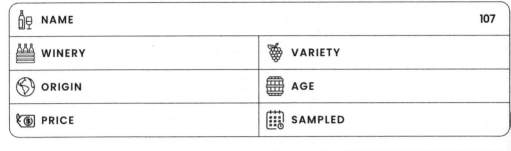	
🍾 **NAME**	
🍷 **WINERY**	🍇 **VARIETY**
🌍 **ORIGIN**	🛢 **AGE**
💵 **PRICE**	📅 **SAMPLED**

COLOR METER

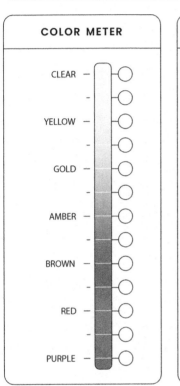

CLEAR —
—
YELLOW —
—
GOLD —
—
AMBER —
—
BROWN —
—
RED —
—
PURPLE —

AROMA AND FLAVOR WHEEL

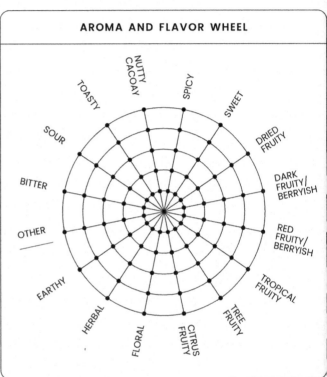

NUTTY CACOAY
SPICY
TOASTY
SWEET
SOUR
DRIED FRUITY
BITTER
DARK FRUITY/ BERRYISH
OTHER
RED FRUITY/ BERRYISH
EARTHY
TROPICAL FRUITY
HERBAL
TREE FRUITY
FLORAL
CITRUS FRUITY

NOTES AND RATING

🔍 APPEARANCE	☆☆☆☆☆
👃 AROMA	☆☆☆☆☆
🍷 FLAVOR	☆☆☆☆☆
🏆 OVERALL RATING	☆☆☆☆☆

🍾 **NAME**			
🍻 **WINERY**		🍇 **VARIETY**	
🌍 **ORIGIN**		🛢 **AGE**	
💵 **PRICE**		📅 **SAMPLED**	

COLOR METER

CLEAR —
  —
YELLOW —
  —
GOLD —
  —
AMBER —
  —
BROWN —
  —
RED —
  —
PURPLE —

AROMA AND FLAVOR WHEEL

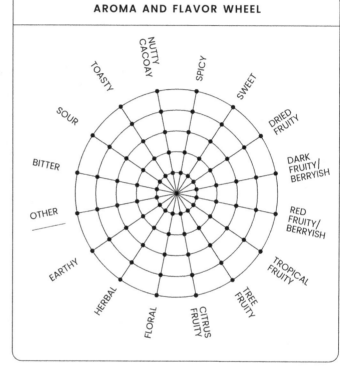

NUTTY CACOAY
SPICY
TOASTY
SWEET
SOUR
DRIED FRUITY
BITTER
DARK FRUITY/ BERRYISH
OTHER
RED FRUITY/ BERRYISH
EARTHY
TROPICAL FRUITY
HERBAL
TREE FRUITY
FLORAL
CITRUS FRUITY

NOTES AND RATING

🔍 **APPEARANCE**

☆☆☆☆☆

👃 **AROMA**

☆☆☆☆☆

🍷 **FLAVOR**

☆☆☆☆☆

🖐 **OVERALL RATING**

☆☆☆☆☆

Thank you for buying our wine tasting journal!

If you enjoyed this journal we would be happy if you support us by leaving a positive review on amazon.

Yours
Laura Lavaux

Made in the USA
Monee, IL
17 September 2023

42904082R00069